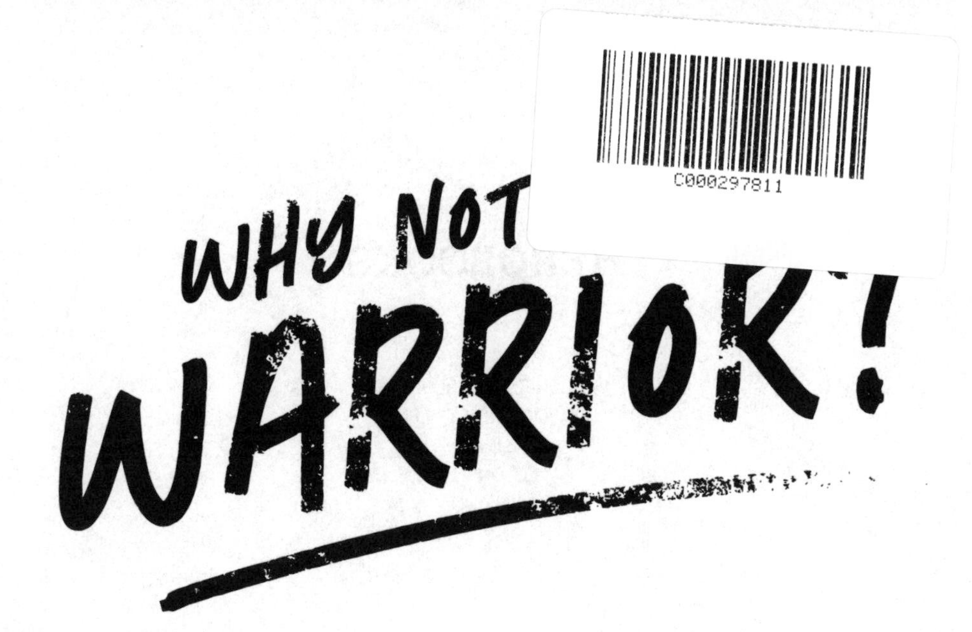

GEMMA O'CONNOR

WITH SINÉAD FARRELL

HEROBOOKS

PUBLISHED BY HERO BOOKS
1 WOODVILLE GREEN
LUCAN
CO. DUBLIN
IRELAND

Hero Books is an imprint of Umbrella Publishing
First Published 2022

A CIP record for this book is available from the British Library

ISBN 9781910827581

Cover design and formatting: jessica@viitaladesign.com
Photographs: Inpho and the O'Connor family collection

DEDICATION

Some people may be lucky enough to have that one person in their life that completely shapes them as a person. This person and role model may come in the form of a parent, a family member, a teacher, a mentor or a friend.
For me, my hero was my mam.
A strong woman who dedicated her life to her family and all things hurling. Her passion for the game and her warmth as a mother made her truly great.
This book is dedicated to my late mother Ger.
Thank you.
I love you always.

CONTENTS

ACKNOWLEDGEMENTS

TWELVE MONTHS AGO, I received a phone call from Sinead Farrell a journalist from *the42.ie* and she had one question for me... would I be interested in writing a book about my career in camogie?

My first thought was... *No.*

Anyone who knows me would probably describe me as an outgoing person, someone who is not very shy. However, those close to me know that I possess both introvert and extrovert characteristics, and hyping up my achievements or speaking openly about my personal life is something that doesn't come naturally.

I was offered this platform and opportunity by Liam Hayes and Hero books to highlight some of my career experiences and personal stories. I looked at the book as a chance to help young people in sport, but also to give the message that it's okay to be yourself.

For this I want to thank Hero Books.

Sinead and I spent many evenings and mornings chatting over zoom calls recounting the highs and lows of my career. Evoking some powerful emotions I encountered along the way. In Sinead, I placed my trust and I want to thank her for her endurance, patience and dedication in piecing together my story.

My journey along the way includes so many people, and I want to give a special thanks to the Defence Forces, and especially sergeant Rena Killeen, my work colleagues, my club St Finbarr's, my teammates past and present, my mentors and coaches, and volunteer members for both club and county.

Thank you to my entire family network and close friends for your kind support. Especially my aunts and uncles, who have been there for me through it all.

Thanks to my parents Geraldine and Dónal for giving me so much. And thanks to my brother Glenn for your endless support and encouragement down through the years.

Finally, to my wife Aoife… thank you from the bottom of my heart for all that you do for me.

Gemma O'Connor
August 2022

*****

JULY 22, 2022.

That was the day I truly understood the depths of Gemma O'Connor, and how she developed into the athlete she became. A person can love a sport, pour every hour into it and walk away with plenty of rewards. Many have been blessed with that life, but with 11 All Stars to her name, Gemma's career surpasses all others in camogie.

I wanted to uncover the reason why she reached a level of distinction that only she knows.

On that day, I asked Gemma how she approaches the art of defending as a centre-back and her response floored me. You'll read about it later in the book, but here's the unedited version of what she said:

'For me, it starts when your'e walking onto the pitch and taking up your position. Everything starts with body language and I like to dominate from the get-go. I think you can give off a sense of attitude and dominance without even touching the ball. You do that through your body language and the way you tog out… the way you dress, the way you stand… and the way you position yourself.

'That 45-yard line and everything in between to the Cork goals… that line is mine. That's how I mark my player.'

That conversation left me with a fuller understanding of how Gemma O'Connor came to be such a distinguished talent. When I agreed to write this book, the fact that much of Gemma's career went by unnoticed by many gaelic games fans wasn't far from my mind. It wasn't until the final years of her inter-county career, when women's sport started really coming under the microscope, that I first came to know of her.

There are many more like me, and if you're similarly unaware of Gemma's achievements, I hope this book will leave you feeling disappointed that you never saw her live in her pomp.

I want to sincerely thank Gemma for trusting me with this project, and for giving me a vivid and honest account of her life. I must credit the invention of Zoom for helping us with that task while she was in Lebanon. Thank you to Paudie Murray and Aoife Murray, Marian McCarthy, Linda Mellerick and Mossie Barrett who also assisted me with recording Gemma's sporting career. Additionally, I hope these pages will bring hope and comfort to those who are struggling with their sexual identity.

To Liam Hayes and Hero Books, thank you for inviting me to write Gemma's book and I hope I was a worthy choice for the job. Thanks to my colleagues at *The42* for facilitating me when I needed to concentrate on the book, and for the feedback they provided when I needed a steer.

My boyfriend Gary has always been and continues to be a source of support and encouragement for me. He played that role many times during this undertaking. And lastly to my family: as the last of the litter, thank you to my parents Fintan and Mary, my brother Stephen and my sisters Sheila and Sarah who all raised me and made me.

Sinéad Farrell
August 2022

PROLOGUE

THERE'S TWO MINUTES left... and we need a point.

Badly.

Something to keep us alive... before time runs out.

The day has moved into the late afternoon.

The sky has suddenly turned grey.

It's what you expect in September; a true sign that time is moving us on from summer's long daylight hours. You start training for the season ahead when the days are short, and if all goes well, you'll still be involved when the nights are starting to draw in on top of you.

And here we are... in the final hour of the 2017 championship, fighting it out with one of our greatest rivals in an All-Ireland final. We're trying to win back the O'Duffy Cup from Kilkenny.

They dethroned us last year. There's plenty of beef between us, and today is a real arm-wrestle that has only mustered up a measly 17 points between us... and time now slipping away.

I'M AROUND THE halfway line in Croke Park when the ball comes to me. This is my kind of range. I can equalise from here if the technique is right.

There's a lot you need to know about a hurley.

For starters, you need to understand that it's an extension of your arm, almost like it's a part of you. You should feel like you're not carrying anything. That's what gives you maximum mobility. Two anatomies intertwining.

The hurley that fits right, and hits the ball right, is nice and light to pick up.

When I was younger, I was precise about the construction of my stick, especially the bás. The centre of the bás is the spring... the pulse of the instrument. I always used one full grip and a half grip, and would never allow anyone but myself to do the wrapping. I always did that sort of prep work in my free time too. I could never understand people gripping up their hurleys at the back of the team bus heading to a game.

A good hurley is one that's light enough to flick... and to hook, but strong enough to execute a good puck and survive the rattle of ash on ash.

I would get attached to a hurley.

It's devastating when a hurley breaks, especially if you've been hurling with it all through the championship. Suddenly, you have to start that whole process... with all its intricacies... again. At county level, you must have at least four hurleys in your gear bag per game.

Three is the minimum. If you're ever caught turning up with only two hurleys, then that's a life sentence in my court. One hurley for playing and one spare is not enough. Maybe you could go to training with two hurleys, but I have three or four hurleys with me at every game.

You assemble your three favourite hurleys in order of preference. You start with your favourite and then you have your second favourite as the first replacement, and so on. The third and fourth hurleys are the back-up sticks in your reserves.

The main frustration in an event like that is when you're handed the wrong hurley. It rarely happens, but if your hurley breaks and someone else's substitute hurley is thrown in to you, that annoys me.

I always wear a helmet to complete the uniform.

My colours are either green or black. But now, in my 16th senior county campaign, I can ease off on those particulars and trust that my ability can wield whatever equipment is in my hand.

Besides, I have a bigger worry on my mind today.

AS I LEAN back to take the shot, I'm preparing to put all my weight on my heavily strapped left knee. The medical wrapping is holding some ligaments in place that were damaged in our semi-final win over Galway.

A grade two tear on my medial collateral ligament… my MCL.

The MCL is a band of tissues. They help to connect the shin and thigh bone, and keeps your knee stable.

Crucially, it's not the ACL… the anterior cruciate ligament, which would have wiped me out before the biggest day of the year. The ACL is a key ligament. It really stabilises the knee joint, connecting the femur to the tibia.

I was blessed, but it wasn't a complete let-off.

I was told the injury would take six weeks to heal… but we only had three to work with. And I squeezed out every minute… every second of those few weeks to make sure I could be fit for selection today.

'Will she play… won't she play?'

There was a lot of that debate in the build-up, but I'm here now… the No 6 on my back. I can't say that I was overly confident before throw-in but, the knee, with all its padding… it's still holding me up after 58 minutes.

Right now, there would be nothing worse than mishitting this shot. Kilkenny are ravenous about retaining their title. They waited 22 years to be All-Ireland champions last year, and they're breathing down our necks every time we get the ball.

THERE'S A RUCK out near the Hogan Stand side of the pitch.

The ball spills to Ashling Thompson.

She transfers it to Laura Treacy.

Laura hits Orla Cotter.

POP, POP… POP!

Orla has the vision to spot me while I'm unmarked in the centre. I'm always trying to work myself into those triangle formations to create opportunities. This one is putting me in a position to try for the equalising point… as the clock goes from black… to red.

Sometimes, you can have too much time on the ball.

But I have just enough precious few seconds to wind up my shot and really have a swing at it. All I can do is trust that my strapped-up knee continues to stay in place through the strike.

When you're looking for a long-range strike, you're aiming to hit the ball through the centre of the bás to get elevation… distance and direction.

A nice fluid stroke that almost sends you twirling.

You know immediately when the connection is off. And you know just as quickly when the strike is right. That's what I'm feeling right now.

The sweet spring.

That's one right in Kilkenny's gut. I jog back to the safety of the Cork trenches to take up my position as the umpire reaches down for the white flag.

Nine points each.

We now have five minutes of injury time to play and Kilkenny are about to retaliate. Me and my knee with its mild cruciate tear.

Start up the process again…

PART ONE

JUST SHORT OF GREAT

At the end of a long and painful final year in Cork's red Gemma surveys the field during the All-Ireland semi-final defeat to Kilkenny. And 2020 also saw the end of a brilliant and sometimes combative relationship with county manager Paudie Murray.

The magnificent three All-Ireland titles in-a-row remained just out of reach on four occasions in Gemma's two decades with Cork. In 2007 (top), it looked promising after Gemma captained Cork to the league title, and in 2016 (below) Gemma receives her marching orders in the All-Ireland final loss to Kilkenny.

CHAPTER 1

A TUBE WITH a camera at the end of it is being lowered down my throat as a tear rolls down my cheek. It's an unpleasant procedure, but that's not why my eyes are watering. Just yesterday, I was warning my Cork manager Paudie Murray that I might be feeling groggy for our first championship match of the 2020 season against Wexford.

'I might even have to sit it out.'

But this shouldn't be a big job. I tell him that this is just a day procedure that has been scheduled for a while and that I'll be in and out in a few hours. I started noticing the problem last year.

Around winter time, I started experiencing some mild left-sided chest pain that was affecting my breathing. The pain was almost crampy, and I was catching my breath. It only lasted for a few seconds in the beginning, but the episodes started happening more regularly and for longer periods of time.

Aoife started getting concerned for me.

'Can you please go to the doctor about it?' she said to me as the pain was getting worse. And so I did. My doctor conducted an ECG, which is a reading of the heart's rhythm and electrical activity, and referred me to a respiratory consultant. I had some tests and scans before coming in today, to the day ward to get this bronchoscopy done. Just a few minutes ago, I was laughing with the nurse about whether or not I could play against Wexford tomorrow.

It's the first year of the Covid-19 pandemic, and the whole season has been flipped to run club activity first in the summer, followed by the county championship in the winter. It's a tight schedule, but I'm pretty sure that this is my last year playing for Cork, so I don't want to miss too much.

Initially, the nurse gave me a fright when she said I wouldn't be fit to do anything for 24 hours, before offering me relief a few seconds later and reassuring me that everything should be fine.

I'm thinking that grogginess and soreness will be the worst of what I'll be facing today. But a lot can change in a few minutes, especially when it's a medical matter.

A SHADOW ON each lung.

That's what my doctor – the respiratory consultant – says my scans have detected. And when he says shadow, he's not talking about the light reflecting off the other organs inside my body.

These are the kind of shadows that have nodules in them… three on one lung and two on the other in my case. They're the kind of shadows that require further medical investigation.

I would happily crank the grogginess up to 10 if it would erase what I've just been told.

Instead, I'm choking back tears.

The doctor has an understudy in the room during all this. So now the doctor, his understudy and the nurse are all looking at my reaction as I try to take it all in. I don't have long to process this news before I'm fitted with a mouth-block and the tube with the camera on it is slinking down through me to have a root around in my lungs.

My mind starts spinning into the darkest places. I start thinking about my mother Geraldine, who died from lung cancer.

The doctor tells me that he doesn't know what the shadows indicate yet. And when I ask for his opinion on what we could be dealing with, he says that there are a number of differentials involved, with cancer and a tumour at the bottom of the list.

He starts listing out the possibilities… auto-immune disease, sarcoidosis… lupus. None of these sound great.

And there are more medical tests to come today.

To make things slightly worse, I start noticing a pain developing in my back as I get my bloods taken and go for an X-ray. The doctor is staying with me throughout the day, reassuring me that the back pain is normal, and has probably been caused by the procedure.

Aoife comes in to collect me.

As we drive home, every lump and bump on the road is ripping through my back. I fall into bed feeling miserable when we get home, only to get a call from the hospital about an hour or two later.

Something went wrong while they were taking my bloods and I have to go back in to redo them. This was supposed to be a straightforward process, and now it's all being dragged out. So, I get my bloods done again, get collected again... and I'm still in agony. I collapse into bed again, but the pain won't let me rest.

Another call comes in.

This time, it's my doctor ringing with more great news. My X-ray has found less than a five percent puncture in my right lung. Well, he did say that the pain could be linked with the procedure, but I didn't expect this. At least that explains why I'm feeling so rotten and uncomfortable.

It turns out that the bronchoscopy caused the puncture. My doctor explains that when they stuck the camera down my throat, they needed to scrape out a piece of tissue from the lungs in order to get a biopsy. He hasn't had a case like this in a while, but this procedure always carries a chance of rupturing the lung.

It's nice to feel rare, but not in circumstances like this. He offers his apologies, but there isn't really much I can say back.

And after all that, my doctor tells me that under no circumstances am I to play the game against Wexford. There's another game coming up shortly, but again, the doctor warns me not to play. All I'll be able to manage is a brisk walk for two weeks. That's a crushing blow in a normal season, but doubly so this year.

This championship has been designed for a shorter period of time, and games are being played week after week. There's not much wiggle room in a bitesize championship to accommodate a crisis like this.

Now that short window is closing in on me.

I START GETTING upset in front of Aoife as the reality of what this all could mean starts to sink in. This is possibly my last season with Cork.

I don't want to miss a second of it.

But If I feel the way I'm feeling now, I'll barely be able to tie my shoes, much less go out and play a game with the limited time we have. I'm already resigning myself to the reality that I'm going to miss half the season.

Paudie steps in to help, and calls up the doctor for my local club, St Finbarr's. He knows my consultant really well and gets my permission to speak to him about my condition. He gets back to me with the update.

But it's not good news.

I could be out for a minimum of eight weeks, and I'll only be fit for a brisk walk or a light run in two or three weeks.

What a way to bow out!

CHAPTER 2

PAUDIE MURRAY IS a mover and a shaker, so when he comes to us in 2016 to tell us that Republic of Ireland and Man United legend Roy Keane is coming to give us a talk, I'm not at all surprised.

Former Cork hurler Niall McCarthy is part of our backroom team this year, and it's through one of his contacts that Roy has agreed to come and speak to us. Roy Keane is one of Cork's greatest sporting exports, and it's such an honour for us to get a chance to learn from him. I'm a Man United fan too, in name at least.

I haven't really followed the game, or the team, that closely since I was younger. I've never been to Old Trafford either, but I would love to travel over to England and catch a game some time. I did meet Steve Bruce once when I was a teenager. The fellow Man United legend came down to my home place in Ballyphehane for some kind of camp and gave me a signed soccer ball. That was such a cool experience for me and now I'm getting the chance to enjoy another encounter with another icon of the club.

Our meeting with Roy is at a closed session where it's just us and him in a room. It's such an intimate setting, unlike those public events where the guest of honour addresses a big crowd of 400 or so people in a massive auditorium. This is just for us.

He's here to talk and take our questions after.

One of the key points that he hits during his time with us is what it means to be an athlete from Cork, and the responsibility that comes with that. In Cork, people can often be a bit cut-throat towards their own. There are some people in Cork who wouldn't be big fans of Roy Keane but as I look at him here and take in every word… all I can see is a complete and utter warrior of Cork birth.

He's talking to us about who we are as people from this county, and I can immediately relate to everything he says. Everyone knows that Roy is passionate about sport, but to sit here and hear him convey all that to us is an inspirational experience. He explains to us how much professional football has developed from the way it used to be when he first started out as a youngster with Nottingham Forest in England. Years ago, they used to be on the lash all the time and going to training sessions half-cut.

Everything was about going out to play a game, having about 20 pints after it, and staying out for a few days. He tells us how that culture needed to change in order for the sport to grow.

Everyone knows of Roy's famous athlete/postman analogy. His belief is that since we don't applaud the postman for delivering our letters, why should we congratulate sportspeople for a job well done?

'I'm a professional soccer player,' he explains to us. 'It's my job. I'm paid to do this. What else am I supposed to do?' He links that with the amateur status of our game and urges us to treat playing for Cork like it's *our* job. There's a minimum standard that you have to reach, but once you get that far, you must push it on from there.

It's interesting how he talks to us about the misconceptions that people have of Roy Keane. They look at him as some kind of oracle who knows all the mysteries of sport. He says that people sometimes ask him questions about what makes a successful athlete tick, hoping that Roy has the miracle answer.

But there's no secret. It all comes down to the same thing… you have to be willing to work harder than everybody else. And you have to be obsessed with what you're doing. It comes down to outlasting your opponent.

That's Roy's main message to us, and we can all understand what he means. But it's not enough to just hear those words and nod your head, even if it is coming from the mouth of someone as influential as Roy Keane. It's about whether or not you have it inside you to carry that out.

There are no mad answers, or scientific explanations. His approach to playing games was that when he crossed the white line, it was *game on*.

Outplay your opponent, hit them hard, dominate possession and do the simple things well. A few people ask questions but I'm happy to just sit here and inhale Roy's words. The whole session lasts for over two hours, and we've gained so much from it.

ROY'S PRESENCE AT this meeting is a great call from Paudie and Niall. He might not be perfect but, since his appointment as Cork camogie manager in 2012, Paudie has done so much for this group. We've won with him, lost with him and he has always tried to set the bar a little bit higher every year regardless of the outcome.

Maybe there were times when he changed things too much and other times when he didn't change things enough, but you would always have to mark him at 150% for effort. His professionalism, approach and desire to do better for Cork camogie is always there.

He always aims for continuous improvement.

*****

I CATCH A glimpse of myself on the big screen as I walk off the pitch with two yellow cards to my name. The image of my face towers over me at my lowest moment. In the GAA world, yellow mixed with yellow equals red and I'm off in the 52nd minute of the 2016 All-Ireland final against Kilkenny.

We're already trailing by eight points when the referee flashes the red card above my head, and now I have to sit back and watch my team lose. That's our All-Ireland defence gone and our dreams of completing a three in-a-row wiped out.

To be fair to my teammates, they manage to claw it back despite being outnumbered, but, unfortunately, it's not enough. Kilkenny, who haven't won a single All-Ireland in 22 years, just have a deeper hunger today and have exposed us for what we are this year.

As we walk back out onto the pitch in Croke Park, defeated, I'm filled with regret… and dealing with my demons. I feel like I've let my teammates down, and I immediately apologise to the girls, and to Paudie.

Everyone is understanding about it and are reassuringly telling me not to give it any more thought. I suppose, what can anyone say in a situation like this?

It's nice to be surrounded by compassionate teammates, but we're at such a low point right now that there isn't much further to fall. Instinctively, you start questioning if you're the cause of all this hurt that the team is feeling?

Is this why we're after losing?

Have I just let the whole team down?

Have I let myself down?

I know how referees respond to me. I don't think I get much of a fair chance out there on the pitch, so I probably can't afford to bring my game too close to the line. After almost every attempt at injecting some physicality into the game, they haul me over for disciplinary hearings.

I'm on first-name terms with most match officials by now. Whenever I'm in trouble, they're like, 'Gemma, come over here... name and number?'

'But you know my name? You're after calling me by my name.

'You've booked me loads of times.'

I'm warned, 'Don't be getting smart now!'

Sometimes there's a bit of humour infused with it all, but that's the typical exchange when referees are giving me the wooden spoon. At the same time, I am only human. I think I've only committed two fouls in this whole game against Kilkenny and I got two yellow cards for it. That's a revealing statistic.

Both incidents happen in the second-half. And to be fair, neither of the cards were really warranted in my view. Okay, maybe after the first offence, when I grabbed the ball at the end of a scuffle... but I didn't deserve to get sent off.

Not long after that first yellow card, I can see that Kilkenny defender Collette Dormer is sizing me up. I can see what she's planning to do. Knowing that I'm on a warning, she just checks my run and I kind of push her out of the way... and that's it.

Two yellow cards in two minutes.

Bye bye, Gemma!

There was no harm done in any of it and I feel that it's my right to defend myself when someone suddenly steps into my path at that speed. But given my track record with referees and the way they pull me up on things, I should know better than to engage with an opponent like that.

Hindsight is a great thing, but when you're out there and your adrenaline is pumping, you can sometimes succumb to frustrations. I have been sent off before... a league match against Tipperary in 2008. That's low stakes stuff though compared to this.

It's fairly s**t to get sent off in an All-Ireland final, especially one that would have elevated Cork to a whole new level of excellence if we won. No-one wants to see their face on the big screen in circumstances like this.

*****

I'D BE LYING if I said I didn't think about chasing an All-Ireland three in-a-row. It's a distinction that sets you apart from all the other teams who tried to scale the mountain, and failed. It's something that hasn't been achieved by a Cork camogie team since the 1970s.

Our team has been divided about whether or not we should talk about it.

But why would you not talk about it? It's something that Cork hasn't experienced in decades. And we have a chance to create our own piece of history. It's something that's there, staring at us straight in the face. You can't just ignore it.

And it's an achievement that's possible to reach.

I was on the pitch when Wexford completed their trio of All-Ireland victories after the 2012 final. Since their triumph came at our expense, the memory is burned into my brain. Back-to-back-to-back is not an unprecedented level of success, and we just have to reach out and grab it.

Wexford clipped us in the 2007 All-Ireland final too before going on that unbeaten run between 2010 and 2012. That's where we get a taste of what's to come from them. In total, they've won four All-Ireland titles in six seasons. We're able for Wexford whenever we meet them in semi-finals or in other stages of the championship, but whenever they get us in Croke Park, we just can't figure them out.

They're a team that has it all... goal scorers, aggression, tenacity, fitness. That's the foundation of a team that gets the three in-a-row quest done. I haven't played against any other team with that kind of mentality.

As players, we try to go out and play like it's any other game, but it's like an athlete going out to win a fifth Olympic medal. Of course, they're going to go out and try to achieve that. And they will openly talk about their dream of completing that mission. So, why can't we talk about going after the three in-a-row?

The mere mention of it has been a topic of debate among the players, which has annoyed me at times.

By not talking about it, you're not setting yourself a goal or target. You're not open about it. You have to treat this kind of achievement differently because it is *different*. It's on your mind so why not just unburden yourself of those thoughts and talk it out with the group? Just let it out.

Three.

In.

A.

Row.

Saying it out loud won't curse you.

Excitement and adrenaline are the qualities that make great teams. If you don't use that and you try to hide it, then you're never really going to reach any of those objectives that you set out. You're just going to become a shadow of yourself on the pitch.

It's ironic because, after the dust settles on our disastrous 2016 season, we make a decision as a group never to mention this season again. We have our debrief, pour over our mistakes, take our learnings and agree to park it.

The season that shall not be named.

Paudie continues to reference it, and we're forced to stage an intervention. 'There's no more talking about 2016!' we tell him. No one wants to talk about it.

There's only so much reliving of situations that you can do to learn from them. I think 2016 ended on such a negative note that no one really wanted to talk about it or think about it afterwards. Fixating on it will only create negativity.

Without the three in-a-row, I don't think I can ever say that I was part of a great Cork team. I can definitely call them very good teams, but greatness is just out of reach without that sequence of superiority. We've had so many opportunities to produce the goods, and have fallen short at the final hurdle.

We can defend our All-Ireland, but I don't know why we fumble the ball on the third go. Is it because players become lacklustre for the third year running? Do we fall into the trap of believing that we'll just get over the line without doing anything different? Does complacency set in? Do we get fed up with the relentlessness of preparation year after year?

I'd probably say yes to all of those questions.

THE PATTERN REVEALS itself again in the 2019 All-Ireland semi-final against Galway. There's nothing between us really, but they're just that little bit better and sharper up front. Their scores came that bit easier than ours. Our defeat probably exposes things about people that I don't like and I feel that they're not producing the effort they gave in 2018... the effort that delivered an All-Ireland title.

A back-to-back All-Ireland, in fact. That might sound very harsh, but I think it's a reality and it's something that has bothered me. These opportunities just don't come around all the time, and it's something that I would love to have achieved. But on the few occasions that it was presented to us, we failed.

I failed.

I thought our standards had slipped a small bit in our conditioning. As captain for the 2019 season, I addressed certain things to both Paudie and the group. But there are only so many times that you can try to reinforce the message before it's time to move on and give people the chance to take action on the warnings.

It's up to management and each individual on the team to absorb the words and do what's right for the team. I was conscious of being excessively negative, and constantly talking about the same thing. So, if you want to talk to a team and say that we need a kick up the ass... or we need to do x, y and z... you can make your case once or twice. But then you have to drop it and stop beating the same drum.

We've won plenty of All-Irelands, no doubt. In fact, Cork has the highest number of senior camogie All-Ireland titles. We climbed up to the top of the charts when we collected our 27th crown in 2017. There was a bit of individual history for my teammate Rena Buckley on the day, as she won her 18th All-Ireland medal across ladies football and camogie with Cork. That made her the most decorated player in GAA history... not just in football or in camogie, and that's a height that no man or woman has ever reached in gaelic games. She's also the first female player to captain her county to an All-Ireland title in both codes.

My other Cork comrade Briege Corkery – another dual servant for Cork – went on to reach that 18-medal honour in 2018. What a haul for both of them!

All of those accolades have their value, but the stamp of a three in-a-row is what eluded us during my career. Just another carcass on the mountain.

*****

THE ERRORS ARE always obvious when a season ends badly. You win or you learn. 2016 is a year to learn. We always feel that we're within shooting distance, but the tell-tale signs show up at different times.

Just before the throw-in for the All-Ireland final, there's a slight bit of controversy on the red carpet after we meet President Michael D Higgins. As part of the pre-match procession, players from both teams are instructed to shake hands as a gesture of gamesmanship before the match gets underway. The Cork team begin walking down the carpet and greet the Kilkenny players one by one.

At some point in all that, my teammate Hannah Looney gets into a small bit of a scuffle with Kilkenny's Collette Dormer. I don't know who instigated it but, I suppose, Hannah is young and maybe a bit naive too. Maybe Collette pushed her and she might have pushed her back? Maybe it was the other way around, but perhaps that brief interlude is setting the tone of whether or not we're really concentrating.

A three-point defeat to Wexford in the group stage of the championship was another lowlight of 2016. It's the only game – apart from the All-Ireland final – that we lost in 2016. We avenge the loss when we meet them again in the semi-final, after extra-time, but on a July day in Wexford Park, we're absolutely diabolical. There's a meltdown afterwards. Tensions in the camp almost descend into a war.

We have underperformed and people are livid. I suppose this opened our eyes to what could happen when everything isn't in place. And perhaps a small sign that things are a bit fractured, or just aren't as good as they should be. I could put it down to the demands we place on ourselves to always win, and the massive expectation that we live with in Cork.

It can be really frustrating when you're not performing and that can cause players to become disjointed. I fear that's what happened to the group in 2016.

Of course, everyone has an opinion then.

Going into the final, we believe we have confronted the mistakes of that defeat, but maybe there's still some cracks that we neglected to look at. Kilkenny are just eager to take us down, and they have exposed our frailties.

There's a real sense of teamwork and camaraderie in their play. Every time they strike a ball, they know exactly who they are hitting it to. We're in with a shout right up to the end, but Kilkenny are just too good. They have the weight of history on their shoulders... 22 years is a long time to go without an All-Ireland title, especially in a county with such tradition as Kilkenny. Perhaps that's a factor too.

2016 is just not a year for the books. You can blame it on a load of things but sometimes years just materialise that way. The team doesn't gel, and doesn't work... personalities clash, and players clash.

Teams will be found out because of it and 2016 was our year of reckoning.

*****

WAKING UP AS an All-Ireland champion is such a sweet feeling. It's the first full day of the celebrations. Instead of regret, you're waking up to a sense of relief. The huge weight of expectation that you felt on the morning of the final has been replaced by a lightness in the group.

We head down for breakfast, and a few... ehhhh orange juices, and get the party started. You can relax and look forward to the winter when you've won an All-Ireland.

But the day after losing an All-Ireland final is wretched.

The reality hits you from the moment you open your eyes in the morning, and sticks to you like chewing gum for the rest of the day. We travel by train for All-Ireland finals, on both legs of the journey over and back. But after the 2016 final, we take the bus back to Cork. It's the first time we change up the transportation routine, and we insist to Paudie that it must be the last time too. A horrible experience that we don't want to repeat if we ever reach the final again. It's another low point to bring a dreary season to a close.

That all said, there are some positives to draw from the 2016 season. We get the chance to work with Niall McCarthy, who comes into join a backroom team that also includes Matthew Twomey. Matthew later goes on to become Paudie's successor as manager in 2021, while Niall is basically hurling royalty in Cork. He comes into our camp with two All-Irelands and one All Star as the sum of his credentials.

The Cork hurlers were a ferocious outfit during the first decade of the 2000s and Niall was a big part of the engine room. Niall is loaded with energy. That's just the kind of person he is, both inside and outside sport. Even if you watched him play, he was always ahead of himself on the pitch. He was gone before he struck the ball, haring around the Cork forward line.

He brings that quality to our sessions and it's a key addition to our set-up. But he doesn't know when to stop. He can't work the controls in his own mind. Always on automatic. I'd be laughing with Paudie, telling him that we're going to be wrecked if he doesn't take Niall away from us.

Niall loves the physicality and the fitness of the game. And it shows when he takes charge at training. He might tell us that we're going to do a 30-minute wallball session, which involves striking a type of speed ball off the wall. We typically use the wallball alley at the Sarsfields club in Glanmire for those kinds of sessions during the pre-season.

It's an exercise that helps improve your first touch, speed work, footwork and hand-to-eye co-ordination. We use racquetballs for that purpose as well. They're small black and blue balls, a bit like the balls used in handball. They have quite a dead weight, which means you have to get into a rhythm in order to maximise their use.

Some people think you have to lash them or put in a bit of force behind it to get it going. But once you understand that the ball has one bounce before you strike it, you realise that getting the ball warmed up and working it into a rhythm is the preferable way to reap the benefits.

Now, you would only ever do a maximum of a 30-minute wallball session.

But Niall turns on the turbo boost when he puts us to work. Before we even start, we do 100 press-ups, and your arms are barely hanging on when it's time to actually start hitting the ball off the wall. But we're blessed with the passion he has brought to our team. He's a really nice guy and really fun to work with too.

Matthew Twomey has a different role. He helps ease the workload for Paudie and does the things that Paudie can't do. Paudie is very managerial in that he just focuses on camogie, tactics and the job at hand. He gets to know the players in his own way, whereas Matthew is very personable and has more one-to-one contact with all of us. He sits down and talks to all the players. It's great for Paudie to have Matthew there providing that service, because it means that he can step back a bit and concentrate on his tasks as manager.

Since Paudie's arrival in 2012, he has always strived to look at how teams prepare in hurling, and mirror what they do with us. Over the years, we have moved from a weekly regime which included two intense sessions along with one less taxing session, to training four nights a week. We have an array of training programmes to follow too. Increasing the volume to four sessions per week is how we progress and evolve as a team.

We tailor our set-up accordingly too. Things change every year in terms of strength and conditioning, and the world of sports science, and Paudie is always sharp in how he reacts to that. He looks to other sports as well for inspiration and guidance on how to make us better. He references teams like the All Blacks, and the Munster and Leinster rugby teams, and breaks it down for us about what they do to win.

He's a big fan of cycling too and makes comparisons there for us to earn the rewards. He takes snippets and nuggets wherever he can, to bring back to our group. Anything, minor or major, that he can incorporate into our training, Paudie will find a place for it.

The training varies so much every year, right throughout the year. There are no periods of repetition. For our indoor sessions, we go to the amazing set-up at the Na Piarsaigh's club. Paudie brings in different coaches to work with us throughout different periods of the season. The versatility keeps everything fresh during the season.

PART TWO

WHO YOU ARE

Gemma's mam and dad Geraldine and Dónal, and (right) Gemma and her dad celebrate together after the 2005 All-Ireland final.

Gemma and her brother Glenn with the Cork football championship trophy and the O'Duffy Cup at home in Ballyphehane after a successful 2018.

Gemma gets a taste of success young (right), at eight years of age at the Cork City Sports in Páirc Úi Chaoimh. And on a night out with friends (above) and (below) with schoolmates from Presentation Secondary School in Ballyphehane.

CHAPTER 3

I'M 15 AND starting to get a bit inquisitive about life.

Sport allows me to do that, and because I play camogie with girls who are older than me, I start exploring the night life a little bit earlier than some of my friends. My mother is a bit hesitant about me maturing through my teens this quickly, but she's a forward thinker so it's all good after a while.

That is, until I get a bit older and occasionally start disappearing for a day or two to go drinking with a gang of friends, or whoever I meet up with. Just to settle her nerves, mam implores me to send her a text when I'm heading out. And, of course, I don't send that message.

Nor do I think to do much else to ease her apprehension. For some of those sessions, I just go off the reservation and don't come home for a bit.

Everyone has a wild phase, but I don't slip too deeply into those bad socialising habits. Sport has such a chokehold on me that I could never stray too far off course. I'm just giving myself a chance to have some fun. It's an exciting time too, getting a taste of the adult social life when you're still a teenager at school.

Taking a look behind the curtain before my time.

Other people my age are still imagining what lurks behind the neon lights above the entrance to a nightclub. I feel very grown up heading out for the night after camogie finals, waving my fake ID like it's an FBI badge as the bouncer nods me in the door. I have a few dealers on that front, one of which is my teammate in the Barr's whose similarity with me extends no further than the fact that we both have black hair.

I'm learning off dates of birth better than my five times tables. It's a lot of fun. I'm out with my teammates who are a bit older than me, which gives mam some comfort about the whole thing.

'Oh please, Ger. We'll look after her,' they promise.

MY TEAMMATES KNOW how to sweeten mam up to let me out. They're having a great time indoctrinating me, and lending me their IDs. But while we're all having a laugh, they are keeping me safe too and mam can collect me later. She appreciates the care they take when I'm out with them. It's better for me to go off for a few hours and do things I shouldn't be doing in the company of people that mam knows, than to vanish with a less familiar group and keep my gallivanting a total mystery from her.

I have another ID from a girl with blonde hair, who is much shorter than me. We're complete opposites in physical appearance, but it's okay because her picture is dark, so that's good enough to at least chance it with the bouncers. And it works… sometimes.

I'm heading into a bar called Sir Henry's, which is one of the biggest nightclubs in Cork at the moment. I'm in the queue, heading up to the bouncer with everything all prepared in my head. I'm watching the people in front of me disappear one by one, waiting for my turn to give a performance.

The bouncer looks at the ID and then looks back at me, giving my face a good scan.

'Yeah, you're not getting in at all tonight!' he tells me.

'Why?'

'You don't even have a picture in the ID, love.'

He hands me back the faceless document as I turn around in shame. My ID had obviously fallen out and I had pulled out another card that had the familiar shape of an ID for the inspection. I retrace my steps and find the damn thing on the ground, but by now, my chance is gone.

Bouncers don't forget the faces of those they've turfed out of the line, and they could hardly forget my mug after mortifying myself a few minutes ago. All I can do is laugh and tell the rest of the girls I'm with to go on and enjoy the night, while I head home. I didn't even get to recite the date of birth without a stutter.

I'm not interested in bushing or sneaking cans in a field, but I do enjoy a few casuals over at a friend's house. I make time for a few tipples in the pub at the Barr's clubhouse as well. That one is particularly challenging with mam and dad knocking about keeping watch. Going up to the bar, the girls often recommend getting the peach schnapps and adding orange to it to cover my tracks.

That should be enough to deceive their beady eyes. I might even start tipping the glass to mam and dad as well... strengthen the illusion that this is just an innocent glass of orange juice.

Sláinte!

Cheers!

Salud!

MY TEENS ARE my most explosive years as both a player and a person. Around 17, 18, and 19 especially, I'm inclined to react if someone says the wrong thing. My sexuality comes up in those moments, and people are trying to weaponise it against me. But even if it's clearly their intention to provoke me just for the fun of it, I still can't ignore the digs.

That's a weakness on my part, but I'm still growing up.

I have to learn the hard way that, sometimes, it's better to simply just walk away. Even on the pitch, this is the time when I'm playing my hardest hurling at the closest point to the edge. And maybe I put a foot over the edge from time to time. I'm a cautionary tale for my younger brother Glenn... an example of what *not* to do. Glenn and I are opposites in almost every way, right down to the way we were born.

It takes a while to coax me out of the womb.

June 7, 1985 is the day I end my mother's suffering and finally agree to come into the world. I was supposed to be born in May, but I just wouldn't budge. One month on, and my mother is in the Erinville Maternity Hospital in Cork city, trying to deliver her first child. Finally. I'm still not playing ball though.

In fact, I'm so reluctant to make my entrance that the medical team have to suction me out. I'm left with a permanent mark on my head from the procedure and my head is shaped like a cone for a while afterwards.

'You took your time to come out,' my mam says about the whole ordeal which was horrific for her. It's an entirely different story with my younger brother. Glenn comes along four years later, and there's no hold up with the second child. He just flies out.

Bingo bango… job's a good 'un.

I suppose those contrasting experiences set the tone for our childhood. Glenn is more easy-going while I'm a bit hyper and have more of a temper. I get the occasional back of the hand and a telling off or two from dad, but there's less of that for Glenn. He gets more lenient treatment, and through observing my carry on, he knows where the line is.

A cute fox posing as an angel.

There's no jealousy between us though, and mam and dad are good to us both. I'm protective of Glenn as we grow up, because he's really quiet, and a gentle child. But he's growing into himself and forming his own personality, so I don't have to worry.

We're all really close as a family. It's a happy childhood for the pair of us. My dad Dónal works as a pipe-fitter and has worked a lot with pharmaceutical companies like Pfizer, MSL and Eli Lilly. Like the rest of us, he loves a simple life, and enjoys meeting my grandad, my uncles and my in-laws for a few drinks. He's obsessed with history too and loves his documentaries.

Mam is a stay-at-home mother and the pillar of the house.

*****

GERALDINE GEANEY IS about 19 years old and she's heading to a dance in town. She meets a guy who starts pestering her. And he continues to pester her until she agrees to give in and give him a chance.

A one-time shot turns into a more permanent arrangement very quickly. So, now it's Geraldine and Dónal… and Dónal and Geraldine.

They're going along as a couple until the age of 24, when they decide to get married. Getting married at 24 sounds crazy to me but this is the 80s, and this is just the norm. I live in an age where people typically wait until their late twenties or thirties before tying the knot. Usually, people go through a few different relationships before finding *their* person and settling down. It's rare that the first love becomes your ever-lasting love.

People are more like penguins in the era of my mam and dad; they tend to find a mate for life in their first partner. Some might even say that Geraldine and Dónal are shoving on a bit to be waiting until their mid-twenties before walking down the aisle. For the first year after I was born they lived in Faranree, before moving into dad's home house with his parents in Ballyphehane.

It's not an ideal living arrangement as my dad's parents are not in great health. His mother suffers from dementia and his father is ill too. That's a lot of responsibility for my mother to take on at such a young age. They're first-time parents by the age of 25, when baby Gemma comes along, before my brother joins us later... and the O'Connor clan is completed.

Raising a family while living with two sick and elderly people sounds very stressful to me. That wouldn't be the deal now. Modern couples marry at an older age and find their own place to live. They might even have their own home and have been living together for a while before they get wed.

Getting married comes second to putting down roots in a place where you can live with your partner on a long-term basis. Some couples might live with their parents for a while to save up some money, but generally, the suggestion of moving in with parents after your wedding would end in divorce proceedings. It makes sense to build a life together by degrees but that would probably be called living in sin in the 80s.

Life for a woman was different back then. The expectation was to marry and give up work to focus on raising a family. Mam had worked in a few different factories before she got married, but my dad was probably on such a good wage that she didn't need to work anymore after that.

MAM LIVES FOR her kids though.

She's involved in everything... coaching our school team, my club camogie team with St Finbarr's, and even going on school tours with me. Everyone else in school gets annoyed when they have to bring the parents along for supervision, but I'm delighted to have mam with me. I suppose she's younger than my friends' parents, so maybe that's part of the reason why our bond is so strong.

We just have such a great relationship that I never go through that awkward phase of feeling like my parents are cramping my style. Some teenagers might feel the urge to reject their parents in order to find their individuality as they grow up, but I never experience that itch, and that's down to the loving environment that's created for us at home.

I love being with my family. Glenn and I even come home for lunch during school… every day to be with our mam. It's a 20-minute walk for me, while Glenn's primary school is practically right next door.

Home is a really small, typical city three-bedroom house where my grandmother, my uncle and the four of us all live together. Six is actually quite a healthy number of occupants compared to the numbers that mam and dad grew up in. There were 11 in my dad's family… eight in my mam's family home on the other side of Cork city.

With that number of people all packed in together, I always wondered where they all slept? Eventually, it's just the four of us as my grandmother passes away and my uncle moves out. It's just a great childhood for Glenn and myself.

The summer is a busy season for me. Every day is filled with being outdoors, playing soccer with my friends around home and packing in as much sport as I can. I'm in a gang with about four or five boys, but I don't have any female friends around here who are into sport until I start playing camogie with a few older girls in the Barr's.

Soccer and camogie are my main sports but I give basketball and taekwondo a spin too. I'm a regular sports nut. I spend every weekend with my mam's siblings and call up to my grandmother's every Sunday for a visit and a feed. I'm not lacking in anything. There's nothing more I could want because Glenn and I get everything we need.

CHAPTER 4

I CAN STILL see Ursula Jacob's goal for Wexford in the 2012 All-Ireland final.

It's probably one of the best scores of all time. It belongs in the company of some of the great goals in hurling and I don't think it will be repeated again.

The ball floats into the path of our goalkeeper Aoife Murray, taking out a Wexford player and one of my Cork teammates on the way. It bounces in front of our defender Jenny Duffy, who is marking Ursula. She already has a step on Jenny as they launch into a sprint... and then Jenny starts to stumble.

All she can do is stretch her stick across in the hope of getting a miracle block or a deflection, but Ursula's connection is perfect. Right in that sweet spot of the bás, with plenty of pace behind the swing. She fires the ball straight into the opposite top corner of the net where Aoife has no chance of keeping it out.

It's just the finest example of perfect ground hurling.

WEXFORD ARE AIMING to complete an All-Ireland three in-a-row today, but that's not a distraction for us. I don't think we're intending to deny Wexford that dream because that becomes a bit of a secondary thing when you're going out to play. You should only ever go out to try and win.

If you're going to think about external aspects deriving from the game, and go out to prevent the opposition from achieving something extra, then you lose sight of what you're trying to do. Their three in-a-row hopes are not on our minds, but

Wexford just put on a show anyway. All of a sudden, they're six points in front and there's no way back for us.

They just block off every path and surround us. They're in total control of the ball when they get it, and can direct their passes at will. They have one thing on their mind and that's... goals. We fail to catch onto their pattern throughout the whole game, or even manage to run interference on them.

We continue to make those mistakes until the end.

You just have to take your hat off to them. That's a special team, with some phenomenal players, and that three in-a-row is not easy to do in camogie. They deserve all the kudos for what they have achieved in that six-year period where they captured All-Ireland titles between 2007 and '12.

Aoife Murray makes a few uncharacteristic errors that day but she produces some fine saves too, as well as scoring a penalty. Shortly after Jacob's goal, Wexford come hunting for the net again. It's another awesome strike along the ground, but this time, Aoife gets her stick behind it with a superb reflex save.

We never trail by much, and the match is fairly even until Wexford take flight in the second-half. They're just so clinical when they get their opportunities. Space just seems to appear for them, although a lot of it is created by us.

They score three goals. We score three goals.

We have a great player in the forwards called Clare Shine, who has been through a hectic schedule this weekend. Clare is a multi-talented athlete who's proficient in ladies football, soccer and camogie. A real all-rounder, and she's still only a teenager. There's a quick burst of pace in her engine with swift, darty movements to keep a defender on their toes.

I see a great future for her in sport. But playing three different sports is a mammoth commitment for her, and for the last two days, she has been attending a training camp with the Republic of Ireland under-19 squad. That's a huge workload for anyone to take on before playing in an All-Ireland final. But Clare has youth on her side and she still managed to play well against Wexford.

She's clearly under a lot of stress trying to keep all her masters happy, and there's the added pressure of playing two sports that have no association with each other. There's no correlation between soccer and camogie, and Clare is suffering for that.

We can all see the potential in her ability; none of that is in question. She's a really nice girl, too. But, from a distance, we can sense that she's struggling with something. It seems like something dark is happening for her in the background and maybe people who aren't that close to her are afraid to ask what's going on?

I've had a few conversations with her about camogie, to try and encourage her, and tell her that I reckon she could be a really good player, if that's what she wants. I really mean that... she could be a major asset for Cork. From a camogie point of view, and a selfish point of view, I'd love to keep her with us long-term, but we all know that she's leaning more towards a career in professional football.

*****

IT'S THE END of the 2010 season, and Denise Cronin is stepping down as manager of the Cork camogie team after three years in charge. Denise was an experienced member of the Cork panel when I first joined the squad in 2002, and has overseen a successful period in which we won the 2008 and 09 'All-Ireland finals.

The 2008 triumph was especially satisfying as we downed the defending champions – and our tormentors – Wexford along the way.

It's a fine June day when we make the trip to New Ross for a repeat of the 2007 All-Ireland decider. And this time, we're the ones with smiles on our faces at full-time. Goals from Síle Burns, Rachel Moloney and Orla Cotter send us back down south with a 10-point victory. That's closure for what we left behind us the year before. It's all the more pleasing that we hit them back with a killer attack on their home turf.

Unfortunately, the 2008-09 period is also a stretch that has to be filled under 'Failed Three In-A-Row Effort For Cork'. We lose our footing at the third hurdle again.

IT'S AUGUST 2010, and we're playing in an All-Ireland semi-final replay against Galway. The drawn game was a high-scoring thriller which ended... Cork 1-17 Galway 3-11. But today's rematch is a dower contest that produces just 19 points between us and zero goals.

Galway are three points clear at half-time but we restore parity after the resumption and eventually edge ahead.

We trade scores in a tense game of tennis, and as the final quarter comes to a close, Galway have a one-point advantage over us. Our All-Ireland title, and three in-a-row tilt, is slipping away.

The referee awards a free to us.

One last chance to score an equaliser. It's around 65 metres from the posts which is my kind of territory. I'm not a natural free-taker, but my pucks can travel long distances which makes me an option for opportunities like this.

It's important to have a routine for striking a free and I have mine from when I was a more regular free-taker as a younger player. I'm working my way through the steps now and locking eyes on the target.

I make sure not to stand too close to the ball, because I feel like I smother myself when I step into it. So, I place the ball, take three steps back and I bend over it rather than stand over the ball.

I take about four looks up at the posts.

And then, I have to get the ball at shoulder height before making contact, because I sometimes have a habit of hitting the ball low, meaning I'm striking the ball from the hip instead of hitting it from my shoulder. Some hurlers and camogie players place the ball at the midpoint between their two feet and stand quite close to it.

Every artist has their own approach.

The lift is the most important part of my routine, even more so than the strike that's coming. If the lift is too low, you nearly have to go under the ball to hit it... and if it's too far forward, you're reaching for it. Every measure must be on point to get better direction and accuracy. I always jab lift the ball too, which is effectively scooping the ball up off the ground in one fluid motion before the swing.

The other type of lift is a roll-lift, which involves placing the hurley over the ball and smoothly motioning the stick forward slightly and then reversing back to flip the ball up onto the bás of the hurley. Both are useful, but I prefer the jab technique.

And once the lift is at its correct level, I take aim and shoot.

I go through the ritual against Galway and give it my trademark forceful swing to try and level the game. But it's not enough. The ball trails off to the wrong side of the posts... the celebrations begin in the Galway camp.

Another attempt at three in-a-row history goes up in smoke.

I can see my effort curl off to the right with the way I've stepped into it. To get the opportunity of scoring the equaliser and then fail to convert… a disastrous way to bow out. Defeats like this sit in my stomach for a bit as the moment replays on an endless loop in my mind.

And the post-mortem begins…

If I had only struck the ball from another angle… we would have snagged a draw. We could even have won with the way we were playing down the home straight of the tie.

We were playing with a good rhythm… we could have changed the outcome of the result if we had a few more minutes left to play with.

Bargaining with the shoulda… woulda… couldas… but it's just not to be this time.

I'm eventually reaching acceptance now.

In match situations, I recover quickly from setbacks. If I feck up, or my player beats me to the first ball, I have the facilities to park the mistake, move on and reset. I don't dwell on it. I just learn from it and use it to help me attack the next ball.

A free in the last minute of the game is a different scenario though. There are no more minutes left for you to do a right that corrects the previous wrong. There's no antidote for the last error before the final whistle.

It hangs on in your head until time moves you on to something new.

*****

THREE YEARS ISN'T really enough for a management team to build anything solid with the squad. Somebody doing a three-year stint, and then somebody else doing another year or two years… I don't believe that really works.

We need some consistency at the top table.

Even if you've won the All-Ireland or achieved something significant in that time, I think the team needs something more stable. You probably need three-to-five years at least to develop structures and form a bond with the players. For 2011, Joe O'Brien of the Glen Rovers club took over as Cork manager and if I'm being honest, that appointment just didn't work out. I don't think the set-up was right that year.

IT'S NOW 2012, and Paudie Murray has been handed the reins. I've always known the Murrays. Their family comes from West Cork which is predominantly football country, and the birthplace of Sam Maguire. His home is just up the road from Murray's place. They come from the parish of Kilmichael and their address is Dunmanway.

There's a big flock of them... six boys and five girls. I've hurled with Aoife for years, and it's through Aoife that I have come to know her brother Paudie very well.

Paudie and I have something of a love-hate relationship.

We are perfectly able to... mildly, bawl each other out of it and not hold any grudges afterwards. He is well used to me and I'm used to him.

We always give one another the chance to have their say, and we don't treat each other with disrespect. I suppose the establishment of a long-term friendship is key to ensuring that lines are not crossed on either side. He's known me since I was 15, so we've had years to get to understand one another's ticks and idiosyncrasies.

We don't go for each other's throats in a malicious way though. We never say anything that can't be unsaid. We thrash it all out, give everything a good rinse, and come out the other side with our skin and bones intact.

He's in charge and he makes the decisions. I must fall into line, even if he decides to proceed with a plan that I have objected to. There are so many occasions where we have thrown our wrath over and back. We push each other to get the best out of each other, all in the name of Cork camogie.

Other relationships might buckle when one bites at the other, but Paudie and I would never allow that to happen. I'm not afraid to speak up to him and he's not afraid to be challenged. He's equally not afraid to ignore me and trust in his own convictions.

Sometimes, after a heated exchange, I might go up to Paudie and relieve the tension with a comment to lighten the mood... 'You're very cranky today!'

That's all that needs to be said to kick off the laughing and joking between us again. We're both fiery characters but the respect between us always outweighs the ego. It's important as a player to have your say too, and that it's not always a one-way dynamic where the management just dictates to the group and there's no facility to offer a response.

A team doesn't have to operate on such strict lines in order to be successful.

Players need to feel free to communicate their views because, at the end of the day, they're the ones who are out on the pitch. Paudie can only come as far as the white line. He can't play the game with us, or for us. We need to know that we're equipped to solve our problems between us as players, without turning to Paudie for instruction every time.

It's also important to be able to square away any disagreements and not to fall out over them. You just have to be as professional as you can about everything. It's in this kind of environment where successful camogie teams are forged.

I work in the Irish Defence Forces and the military is built on similar structures. Everybody has a boss, no matter what rank you are. From the chief of staff who deals with the Minister of Defence right down to the very basic recruit.

Everyone has someone to answer to.

There's a direct chain of command, and you don't bypass the order unless an issue like bullying crops up. Recruits report to corporals, who report to sergeants, who report to the platoon commander, who are answerable to the company sergeant or company commander. We all have our title, we all have our place and everything is inter-connected.

No one can exist or succeed without the other.

Paudie is our company commander and we are his troops.

IT'S THROUGH MY club St Finbarr's in Cork city that Paudie and his brothers first found their way into hurling. They came to the city to attend St Finbarr's College in Farranferris as boarders. Their uncle was also a student in Farranferris where he achieved Dr Harty Cup and All-Ireland colleges success. Paudie became friends with someone from the Cloughduv club, which is the first club the family hurled for. Paudie also befriended day pupils who came from the Barr's club, and he later transferred there along with his brothers, while Aoife and their sister Emer remained with Cloughduv.

He got married and became a city dweller, and a sticky corner-back for the Barr's.

His brother Kevin joined Paudie in becoming a Barr's man too and he found his feet as a corner-forward. Paudie has brought Kevin in as part of the Cork backroom team. Damien Murray, their other brother, has also come on board along the way as a stats person, and one of our runners. Runners play an important role in modern GAA teams. They have various jobs to carry out during games, and form an important link between the players and the management. When required, the runners will race out onto the pitch to deliver instructions from the sideline, whether that's a tactical switch, a word of encouragement or a stern warning to get your s**t together.

Managers still roar in what they need to say... they don't stay mute just because they have runners in the backroom team. But when the big games roll around in the larger venues, and the crowd noise drowns out every other sound on the pitch, a manager's voice just gets lost in the volume. So, instead of screaming until their tonsils are raw, they deploy a runner with the messages that we need to hear.

That's where someone like Damien comes in to do a job. Runners also bring in water during the game and are on hand to give you a replacement hurley if one gets broken. You'll see Damien whizzing up and down the line, ready to jump into action whenever he's needed.

Another one of our stats guys is a first cousin of the Murrays. The Murrays are like the Von Trapp family of Cork camogie.

I know how they operate... their heart is in the right place, and I know what they're going to bring to the table.

*****

PAUDIE'S ARRIVAL USHERS in a new era for Cork and it's thanks to a Barr's woman that he agrees to come on board with us. Marian McCarthy is the Cork camogie chairperson and she bleeds blue for our club. Her contribution to the sport is so great that few people like to let her down when she asks something of them.

She's on a committee which has been tasked with finding the new Cork camogie manager, and Marian has her eye on Paudie. He's in charge of a men's football club team in Cork when she makes her approach... and Paudie is quite happy in his role as manager of the Doheny's senior footballers. But Marian wants to divert his services to us and he doesn't want to disappoint her.

Paudie can immediately identify what's missing in our set-up. He sees the renovation work that needs to be done, starting with the casual, happy-go-lucky atmosphere in the group. In his view, a county camogie team should match the standard of a county hurling team and he's shocked to discover that our set-up is not in line with our Cork hurling counterparts.

Fitness levels, and standards of training… grounds, facilities… and strength and conditioning levels are the key features that Paudie wants to target and improve in our group.

We know we have something a bit different with Paudie in charge.

He gives us something to focus on for the future. It's exciting to think about the prospects. We have a good base to work from too. One thing you can give us kudos for is our ability to consistently show up every season. Yes, we must go without that three in-row achievement, but sometimes reaching a peak can be debilitating in the long term.

Things didn't go as well for Wexford after they won their three in-a-row. They went a bit downhill after they beat us in the 2007 final too. Regardless of how our seasons end, we don't slip too far off the top step.

We're competitive every year. It's crucial to have that hunger in the group now that Paudie is taking over for what will hopefully be a substantial stretch.

*****

AT CORK CAMOGIE training, players are responsible for setting standards, driving standards and taking action when we're falling short of those standards. If errors start creeping in, someone must take the initiative to call that out.

We're blessed in Cork to have players who naturally assume those authoritative roles. We have the usual suspects who will, in those instances, put up the hurley, call the team in and release the rallying cry.

'Girls… this isn't good enough.

'We've had five dropped balls!!

'We need to cop on.'

I'm not afraid to be the player who will pull the group in to say what needs to be said. That's not to suggest that there's no room for fun at training. There's a fine balance between having the craic… and letting sloppiness compromise our efforts. Once the session starts, we switch on straightaway and start getting serious.

If there's a joke to be had in the middle of training, then let it happen and enjoy it for the moment, before parking it and refocusing again. That's important too. People get superstitious about sticking rigidly to routine, almost to the point where it becomes joyless.

That just sucks the life out of the player before training even starts.

There are times where someone keeps fecking up at training, and we all start laughing because it just becomes funny. We just have to judge the situation in the context of where we are in the season. If it's just a training session in the league, we can treat those moments with a bit more humour.

But if we're in the depths of championship, we have to take a sterner approach to errors. But, overall, if we feel our standards are slipping, we call that out ourselves.

Attitudes towards training have changed so much over the years. The time before a session starts was once your own to spend however you like. Players generally spend that prelude having chats out on the pitch or having a light puck about. Now, every second from the moment you arrive in the dressing-room, is dedicated to something.

If training is scheduled for 7pm, I'm walking into the dressing-room at 6.30pm. There's a bit of chit-chat with whoever else is there and then the pre-habilitation work begins. Pre-hab is a cornerstone of modern training. We're preparing our bodies not to get injured.

It's a prerequisite to get stretching done before training and to get band work done as well. That involves getting a stretchy resistance band and gripping it around your outstretched foot and giving it a good tug. Out on the pitch then, we all take five shots from the 13-metre line, the 21-metre line and the 45-metre line… and then swap sides.

That's the pre-training routine, before getting into the meat of the session. I try not to be tense about the pre-training stuff but I don't clown around too much either.

Strength and conditioning has revolutionised our sport as well, and it's transforming the general body shape of players. From 2002 to '04, when I first started playing with the Cork seniors, I was very lean. But after joining the army, I tried to put on as much conditioning as I could.

That all derives from the circuits, weights, running, and gym work that we do. I've put on some bulk and muscle mass as a result, although part of that physical change is down to how I'm developing naturally as a human being as well.

*****

THE 2012 ALL-IRELAND final doesn't end well for us, but maybe that will amount to a positive for us? Maybe falling short in the final is the incentive we need to follow Paudie's instruction and trust in the plan that he has for us?

Stuttering over the line and winning the All-Ireland with big deficiencies in our camp would deny us the motivation to improve. However, we do end the year as league champions after beating Wexford.

At least we can say that we beat them in one final that year.

The league is funny because even though you go out with the intention of winning it, it really means nothing. It's an opener… a little peep into what's in store for the rest of the season. But winning the league doesn't *mean* anything. You see that in football and hurling too.

What happens in the league is completely different to what happens in the championship. You can't always trust the form that teams are in during the league. You really see what everyone is made of when they step onto the summer championship grass.

By the same token, losing the league final doesn't derail your season. We've lost league finals and won them too, but neither of those outcomes define us. For us in Cork, momentum and progression are what characterise the best of what we have.

Sometimes by winning things like the league, you don't have anything to actually compare it to because you're after *winning*. Losing really identifies what you need to work on… what gaps need closing. You learn more from losing than you do from winning, but then again, you don't want to fall into the habit of consistently losing.

If you start developing that pattern, then you're not learning anything.

You have to box clever and then start switching on when it's time to get serious in the championship. There's no real time for complacency once we park the events of the league.

2012 IS ALSO THE year Cork camogie moves into a new training base that's exclusively for us. Typically, county teams in ladies football and camogie don't have a settled place to train, and are forced to scramble about for pitch availability all the time.

We're fortunate that we have always had a good stable base for pitches, starting with the Mardyke where we trained consistently for a few years. Then it was onto Curraheen, and later CIT. We sometimes use other pitches in between for whatever reason, but those occasions are rare. We might want to use other pitches for a specific reason.

And now, on Castle Road near Blackrock Castle in Cork city, we have a dedicated playing grounds for the county camogie team. It's a lovely pitch and it's where all the club championship games are played. It would be a fine venue for county championship games too, and the only reason that we don't stage games there is because there's no stand. But work is ongoing to change that.

*****

IN THE FINAL moments of that 2012 All-Ireland final, I end up having an argument with one of the umpires behind our goals on the Davin end of Croke Park. With the game already over, I'm remonstrating with him over a decision that didn't go our way.

It's normal to feel frustrated.

If you don't have that, or fight for your team, you're at nothing.

No player gets anywhere by not showing any want to win or dispute something when you feel that you're wronged. Even if all hope of winning is gone.

The 2012 season just doesn't end as we had hoped, but it's still a relief to know that we have a settled leader in Paudie.

We can feel good things are coming for us.

2012 isn't all bad for me though… not after getting a special notification on Snapchat that changes my life forever.

CHAPTER 5

AN IRISH NAME pops up on the screen when I open the Snapchat app.

AoifeNi wants to add me as a friend.

And who is *AoifeNi?*

Well, she's from a place called Knockavilla in Cork.

I FIRST HEAR of the place when a close neighbour of mine, Barbara O'Connell invites me to play soccer for Knockavilla Celtic. Barbara is a sports journalist and she asks me and a few other girls in the city if we have any interest in having a go?

My first thought... where is Knockavilla?

Well, it's a place in West Cork, which is about half an hour outside of Cork city. This is a big county and West Cork is another planet compared to where I live. Anyway, they play in a West Cork league during the winter.

I'm thinking that it might be a bit of craic... and something to do during the camogie off-season.

A lot of my friends from Ballyphehane end up playing for the team too. Compared to camogie, it's a far more relaxed weekend activity. Matches are played on a Sunday morning and we wash it all down with a few pints after.

AoifeNi is also playing for Knockavilla, and her father is our manager.

I've always had an interest in soccer and I grew up playing with some of the lads in my local area. I played in school too, and with Wilton United FC. But again, everything was clashing with camogie, and camogie was my priority. For me, with sport, I was very tunnel-visioned and I just wanted to play camogie.

No other sport could splinter my attention.

I was never willing to sacrifice any part of my game for anything else. I played in Munster schools and would love to have played at a higher level of some description, but my compass always brought me back to camogie.

*****

IT'S APRIL OF my first season with Knockavilla, in 2012, and we're in the Ladies Cup final. But playing with Knockavilla is still just a bit of craic… I'm not taking it seriously. Results are going pretty well for us though, and I knock in a few goals along the way, playing as an attacking midfielder.

We're currently second in the league, trailing the current leaders Drinagh Rangers by just two points. Knockavilla are the reigning champions in this cup competition and we're aiming to retain our trophy against Inter Kenmare, who are a South Kerry outfit competing in this competition for the first time.

A win today would bring us halfway to a league and cup double. We're playing in Darrara College in Clonakilty, and it looks like we're heading for penalties. No goals at full-time, although both sides had a few chances.

I hit the post in the first-half from a long-range shot, and had another chance later in the half that was saved by the Kenmare goalkeeper. My teammate Barbara O'Connell came close to breaking the deadlock too, but her header from a corner was cleared off the line. Kenmare grew into the game after the interval, and created a few goal-scoring chances of their own. They hit the woodwork too… twice, in fact but, thankfully, they don't hit the net. We're still at 0-0 in extra-time and a penalty shootout is on the cards. But before we get to that final resort to decide a winner, Barbara is fouled in the Kenmare penalty area and we have a chance to seal the win.

We don't have a set penalty taker and, as the referee points to the spot, nobody wants to volunteer for this one. Everyone is looking around to see if someone else will put up their hand… and put an end to the tension.

I offer myself up for the job. I'm naturally right-footed, although I can deploy the left foot in an emergency. For this kick, I'm keeping the effort simple. I put lots of power behind the shot and drill the ball into the bottom left-hand corner. For the first time today, with about five minutes left in the game, the net starts swishing as we take the lead.

It's a precarious time to pick up a one-goal advantage, but we manage to hold on. Celebrations begin as the trophy is presented to our captain Aisling Lynch, and just as we've done after all our games so far, we head off for a pour after.

We complete the league and cup double in June, defeating Drinagh Rangers 2-1 in a play-off. Again, my penalty-taking services are required just before half-time, and again, I convert the opportunity. That goal was an equaliser after Dringah striker Catriona Moloney struck for the opener in the 20th minute. Caoimhe Creedon, who also plays for the Cork ladies football team, grabs the winner for Knockavilla in the second-half to deliver another trophy for us. It's a first-ever double for Knockavilla after almost a decade competing in the West Cork League.

It's great to hit those marks with Knockavilla, but it's important for me to assure Paudie that playing soccer won't interfere with my camogie. I have to have that conversation with him when a crossover occurs between the seasons. The soccer league is bleeding into the camogie season slightly, but there's nothing to worry about.

'Don't have a heart attack, now,' I say to Paudie, 'but we have a game next week with Knockavilla...'

'Oh, I used to play soccer for Castletown Celtic...' he replies. It turns out that he's played the sport before. In short, he's cool about the whole thing. But it's still important for me to check in with him about all this, because fixture clashes are a big problem for some of the dual players in our squad.

And here I am, asking him if I can play a West Cork League soccer game. Once I have those games squared away, I can get down to the serious business with Cork camogie. There have been times where I've contemplated the road not travelled. I grew up with a ball at my feet, and maybe I could have pursued a future in soccer. That said, however, I don't think there is anything that could pull me away from camogie.

*****

SO, *AoifeNi* IS a teammate and someone I know.

A friend of a friend, really. I can't say that I know her much more than that.

We first speak at a mutual friend's party in 2012. It's pretty packed but we manage to peel off and start chatting. As with most parties, the crowd eventually makes a move towards town to keep the night going.

On the way in, I start thinking to myself, wondering what *AoifeNi's* story might be?

Thankfully, I don't have to question things for too long.

We connect instantly. We start texting… meeting up, and begin to figure out if we fit into each other's lives.

As time goes on, *AoifeNi* becomes more than a Snapchat acquaintance to me. She's Aoife NÍ Chrualaoí, and we share a lot of common interests.

We both love food and cooking.

We love sport too.

She doesn't play camogie, but she soon starts attending my games. She's there in Croke Park to witness the defeat to Wexford in the 2012 All-Ireland final. Already, she's signing up to suffer through the cruellest sides of sport with me.

Friday nights are for *us* in the early days. Aoife works as a teacher, and when school's out at the end of the week, we hang out… maybe go for a bite to eat and have a glass of wine. We just work well as a pair from the beginning.

WE HEAD OUT to Heir Island, to Aoife's dad's house, for our first proper time away together. It's cold and sunny as we sit outside, off the southwest of Cork, shooting the breeze over cheese, crackers and wine.

You find out quickly enough if a person is annoying or not, and so far… I like what Aoife's about.

We're completely different in every way.

She's calm… I'm hyper.

I'm tall… she's small.

I wear completely different clothes to her, and the same with jewellery. I sleep soundly the night before our wedding, and she can't get a wink.

She's non-confrontational, but stubborn too. She tries to prolong arguments, but whenever we row, I don't allow her to let things fester. We have to deal with it now. The issue must be discussed and then pack it away.

There's just one tricky thing to navigate during that period… Aoife's not out.

Now, I never officially came out. Straight people never have to confirm their heterosexuality and I just never stood up and announced to the world... 'My name is Gemma O'Connor and I'm gay'.

But, at the same time, my sexuality has been known to my friends and family since I was 17.

Aoife hasn't reached that point just yet with her family, but she assures me that there's nothing to worry about with them accepting her for *her*. We keep our relationship a secret for a while until she's ready to unveil that part of herself to others.

We have mutual friends but we don't tell them either for a bit. As time goes on, we just allow people to put two and two together, and figure out the easy equation. You don't necessarily have to announce... 'Oh we're together'. We just allow word to spread.

Sometimes, I do find myself resenting that a bit... the pressure to verify a same-sex relationship. If I was straight, I wouldn't have to do this.

That inequality does cross my mind at times.

I just don't understand the obsession that people have about who other people get to spend their time with, or who they share their life with. That's more than just an Irish issue, it's a human one too. The treatment of people in same-sex relationships is so varied all over the world.

In some cultures, you can only do one thing and that's be with a man or a woman. You have to flee to another country to earn the right to be who you are. Other cultures allow you to be as free-spirited as you want, and we have an open enough country here in Ireland which I'm very grateful for.

*****

I'M ABOUT 17 or 18 when my phone starts ringing on a Saturday morning.

Mam is up and about, while my dad is still asleep in bed. I don't recognise the number but I accept the call anyway. The conversation is brief but goes on long enough to render me speechless. The person on the other end of the line gives me their name and I wish I wrote it down.

'I'm a freelance journalist... are you gay?'

That's all I can hear during our exchange.

They could still be speaking on the other end of the line, but I'm too stunned to take in anything else. All I can manage for a reply is to ask where they got my number, before panicking and explaining that I have to go.

I can't comprehend what has just happened.

I have no clue why they're calling, and inquiring about my personal life. Another pitiful example of someone needlessly obsessing over the romantic lives of others.

I can only assume this is a limp attempt at a story. And for some reason, the personal matters affecting Gemma O'Connor are gossip fodder.

PART THREE

TO WAR

Receiving her 11th All Star award in 2018 was one of the most memorable occasions in Gemma's career (top and middle), and touring New York with teammates and opponents (below with the 2018 team) was always a unique opportunity to get to know an amazing group of athletes.

The 2008 All-Ireland victory over Galway (left and middle) was one of the very special days for Gemma. And throughout her career Gemma forged a strong and unbreakable relationship with Aoife Murray (below, introducing Gemma to President of Ireland Michael D Higgins).

CHAPTER 6

IT ALL STARTS with body language.

My movement, my posture, my presence... every way my body moves must communicate a clear message to my opponent. This is the 45-yard line and everything along this border, from this point all the way back to the Cork goal... is mine.

Every blade of grass in this zone belongs to me.

This is my territory... your torture pit.

Enter at your own risk.

And when you see me walking out onto the pitch and approaching you as I take up my position, that warning should be clear. You should be able to sense it through my attitude before even touching the ball.

It should cover you like perfume.

Even the way I dress and tog out should reinforce my superiority.

I'm here to dominate from the first whistle.

WITH CORK, WE have game plans and tactics to abide by.

But when I'm marking a player as a centre-back, I always have important calls to make to keep the house safe from intruders. I try not to get too sucked into the idea of marking a player instead of the space, because if I mark the player everywhere on the pitch, I then create a massive hole down through the centre of our defence. Too much space threatens our defence.

If the opposition breaks our lines, my absence leaves us exposed and they can rush us before we even get a chance to re-organise our formation. So, if my opponent wants to stand on the '45' or maybe a step or two above that in the direction of the 50-yard line, then that suits me.

We can dance.

Hip to hip... shoulder to shoulder.

But if that player wants to stray off to the left or right of the '45', or decides to wander out towards the middle of the field... I'll let her go. That player poses no danger to me or to my team from there.

Yes, they might have freedom to gather the ball and play it further into our defence, but it's much safer to give them that luxury out there than for me to follow the player out of position and create a free runway for the opposition to charge through.

My responsibility is to control that spine of the Cork defence, and to protect it at all costs. It's the way I operate, and I've been finessing that formula for years. You begin to learn your role fairly quickly and you begin to learn what's important and what's not important when you're out there on the front line.

So, when people take up positions like centre-back for the first few games, they might get sucked in by the 'unimportance' of marking a player out the field rather than staying and controlling their area. That's the way I see it, and I think people can get deceived by man-marking duties and spend an excessive amount of time following their player around the pitch.

I enjoy watching American Football and I think the centre-back position is almost like the quarterback on an American Football team. From the centre-back position, I have a full-scale view of the pitch.

Our midfielders and wing-backs are all in my eyeline and one of my jobs is to create plays with those players whenever I can. The quarterback is a creator of plays too, and if you take the quarterback out of the game, you're taking away a massive part of the team.

There's no one particular player or team that I'm fond of.

Of course, Tom Brady is the most famous and consistently brilliant quarterback there is, but I'm just drawn to the craft. I learn from the sport as opposed to the person.

When I was young, I had a thing for the Miami Dolphins but now, I just watch whatever game is on television. I really like the sport because it's tactical and the way the plays work is very intelligent. You're trying to outsmart the other team all the time.

I try to look at other sports and take snippets of inspiration from anything that's relevant to camogie.

Being an effective centre-back sometimes means sacrificing your own game for the safety of the team. But it's always about making the most sensible call for your team. Allowing the player you're marking to create a scoring opportunity out near the wing is a low-risk decision.

It's always preferable to let them off to score a point from out there, than to concede space down the middle.

You're always trying to find the balance of what's right for the team, and what's right for you. There might be some games where you have to follow a player, and someone else might step into your position to protect the spine.

And, of course, I'm sure there have been some occasions where I went too far forward or too far back from that zone. There were some games that annoyed me and I was too far back, which is playing the position too protectively. You have to be able to go forward and be available to get involved in the play… but you're too far back to do that.

I can judge the play very well, and I know when it's the right time to close up shop. I'm not the perfect defender but my role as a centre-back is to read the game, supply the ball and be available to the 'keeper and the rest of my backs at all times.

I think I do the job well.

You're like the midfielder of the backline and it's up to you to call it.

It's essential to be vocal if you want to fulfil the brief of a centre-back. It's like playing the role of the goalkeeper in that sense. If you're a 'keeper and you're not vocal, that's about 50 percent of your job lost. As a centre-back, you're calling on your forwards, your midfielders… the rest of the backline, and you're talking to your goalkeeper constantly.

It's all about communication, which is the case all over the pitch but there are certain pillar positions on the pitch where communication is all the more vital. Centre-back is one of those positions.

Centre-back is probably my best position.

Some might say that my skills are better suited to a position where I'm facing the ball, but the No 6 jersey is home to me. By the end of 2018, after a reasonably solid year, I'm collecting my 11th All Star.

It's my fifth one as a midfielder, to go with the five I've earned as a defender and one as a forward.

WINNING AN 11th All Star is brilliant and puts me in exclusive company. We play a team sport but it's really nice to have your own individual accolades.

Kilkenny hurling legend Henry Shefflin has 11 and the iconic Cora Staunton from Mayo has 11 too. Both of those players are widely accepted as some of the best players of all time, across all four codes in the GAA.

For the game itself, it's nice that camogie has a representative with that number of All Stars, since ladies football has one and hurling has one. Briege Corkery has 16 All Stars across football and camogie.

It's important to me that I'm able to put camogie on a pedestal in that regard and be their representative, who has a level of longevity and success that's on par with other players in the GAA.

*****

IT'S THE 2007 All-Ireland final and we're facing Wexford.

I'm starting at midfield, marking Bronagh Furlong who is on the Irish athletics team and is aspiring to reach the Beijing Olympics next year. She's a brilliant middle-distance athlete, and going into the game, I'm worried about the prospect of haring after a track specialist. But camogie demands a different kind of fitness.

There's no running track here, and no one will be getting a medal for running laps. I have a big engine too, and I'm at my peak as an athlete. Between my sport and my work in the army, training is my life.

I'm doing stuff that others aren't and that gives me an advantage on everyone else. In the army, we do a lot of cardio type circuits and upper body stuff. We also do block runs as part of our fitness programme, which is never anything less than 10km.

I'm running against men as well, which adds another dimension to my training.

I could have a day of that training with the army and then go to a session with Cork that evening. I sometimes run from the barracks I work in to Ballyphehane with a weight on my back. But I know how to keep everything in proportion and avoid burnout through overtraining.

When I get those ratios right, I know that extra training will give me an extra gear to switch into in the latter stages of the game. I'll have enough juice in the legs to outrun, and outwork anyone else. It's that kind of work that makes me more comparable with an athlete like Bronagh Furlong on the pitch.

I'M NOT AFRAID of any player that I'm assigned to mark. I relish every challenge that is laid out before me. And I've marked plenty from the elite class of the sport.

When I started off in 2002, I had lots of battles with Philly Fogarty from Tipperary. She was part of the breakthrough team that won a first All-Ireland camogie title for the county in 1999, and went on to win four more All-Ireland medals with Tipperary. But there was no love lost between Philly and I when we squared off on the pitch.

I've had several encounters with Wexford's Kate Kelly too, and Therese Maher of Galway. These are the kind of players that will give you a real measure of your quality at the top level. I never feared anybody, but I respected their talent.

As long as you recognise their ability, you're in a good place to either match it or outplay your opponent. If you get complacent, that's when you get caught out, and players of this calibre will make ribbons of you.

Today, in the 2007 All-Ireland final... Bronagh Furlong is my assignment.

THE SHOULDER TACKLE is not permitted in camogie but Bronagh and I crack into each other at one point in the game, and almost take each other apart.

I don't know why shouldering is illegal in ladies football and camogie. Moreover, I don't know why people still categorise these sports as non-contact. The multitude of bruises and cuts that I've accumulated over the years are evidence of the contrary.

Don't get me wrong, I think the Camogie Association is trying to tweak the playing rules to progress the game and send it in the right direction. But that stranglehold on the rule changes is still there. They're only holding themselves back by not enabling players to be more physical on the pitch.

I think they should just let it go and give players the license to be more aggressive in matches.

We're top level athletes who are out training four or five nights a week... we're really well conditioned, really aggressive and athletic. We're well equipped to give and receive the hits, so if there are two players running for a ball during a game, why can't you give a shoulder in the hunt for possession?

Obviously, a rule like the shoulder challenge has to be policed to show the difference between fair and unfair shoulders. I'm not suggesting that we allow the game to become dirty or lawless, but we must give women the respect they deserve as athletes, and acknowledge the truth that they're tough and aggressive.

We're not these wall flowers that people might perceive us to be. We're able for more than what the rulebook allows us to do. Our minds and bodies are programmed in much the same way as a male athlete. Men are allowed to shoulder each other in football and hurling, so I can't understand why a similar rule can't be introduced in ladies football and camogie. I think it would improve the game as a spectacle too.

You're talking about women ranging between 11 and 12 stone of athleticism, so why not empower them to shoulder each other for a ball? Maybe not everyone would agree with that view, and maybe some players feel that the shoulder tackle wouldn't suit their game and they would reject such a rule change.

The shoulder challenge certainly doesn't feature in the rulebook in 2007, but Bronagh Furlong and I clatter into each other during the All-Ireland final anyway. That exchange just typifies the physicality and intensity of the game.

They're very physical in the backline, and indeed, all over the pitch. In ways, it's the foundation of their victory.

*****

SOMETIMES, WOMEN CAN be their own worst enemies in terms of progression and initiating change in sport. We're our own biggest obstacle on that score. I'm on the other side of the fence now in 2022, and the shoulder tackle is still prohibited in camogie.

The skort is a similarly divisive subject in our sport.

Debates about its existence come up at various times and then they disappear again. And yet, the skort is still here.

I've always questioned why you would wear skorts, or skirts, while playing any sport. We see those kinds of garments in hockey and tennis too, and I don't know why women must abide by that attire.

I hated the old pleated skort that had to be pinned on. They absorbed moisture as well which made them a nightmare to wear on a wet day. We had to pin them too, because the clasp was either broken or too big. We also needed to wear shorts underneath the skort to avoid feeling exposed.

They were a nuisance to wear and there was no give in the material. That version of the skort was definitely stupid. Another type of skort was later introduced that was lighter to wear but the shorts part of it didn't offer enough flexibility.

They ripped a lot when you put them on.

That said, I've grown up wearing the skort while playing camogie. I'm reluctant to completely trash something that I've always known.

And the skort that's in the sport now has all the right upgrades. It's much more comfortable and gives you lots of mobility. They're made from lightweight material and the shorts – similar to bicycle shorts – are built into them, making them easier to wear.

Not a wretched pleat in sight.

No restrictive heavy fibres weighing you down.

Maybe I've become institutionalised, but, in a way, the skort does look good when you're wearing it. The shorts are worn in ladies football, but they often look oversized and don't fit as neatly as the skort. Camogie players do tog off well, and maybe the skort is part of that.

I think some county and club players would actually tell you that they like them. If a vote was declared in the morning to decide whether or not we should banish skorts from the game, I don't think it would be unanimous.

Some would vote for shorts and happily part ways with the skorts. But others wouldn't like to end that tradition. In 2018, a motion went before the Camogie congress proposing to replace skorts with shorts, but was resoundingly defeated by 77 votes to 12.

A survey regarding the skort was conducted among camogie players a few years ago too. The WGPA (Women's Gaelic Players Association) which has since merged with the GPA, conducted the survey, and a surprisingly high number of players voted to keep the skorts. There was roughly a 50-50 split in the votes.

I was shocked by that, but then again, the outcome of a voting process can always produce surprises. The opinions that people express don't always tally with how they actually cast their vote. Then again, why go to all that effort to preserve the skort?

Why not just simplify everything for players and allow them to wear shorts? It's more of the aesthetics than anything else that might irk people about the skort.

It almost feels like we have to wear skorts because we're women, even though the men wear shorts. There are pros and cons to it, and it's a bit contradictory in a way. You want to be treated the same as men, and given the same opportunities. It's all a bit funny, really.

It's similar to the controversy involving the Norway's beach handball team, who chose to wear shorts instead of bikini bottoms which are part of the sport's uniform. Arguments around the title of ladies football come into that discussion too. The term 'lady' implies that you have to be a lady to play the sport, which is completely off the mark.

A title like that doesn't capture the intensity and physicality of the sport at all. This is not afternoon tea and I can completely see why people would want to change it. Should we call it women's football?

Or just gaelic football?

Camogie was also given that title because it's women that play it. We're playing hurling, and yet, that word doesn't feature in the description of our sport.

You could talk about women's sport all day.

Nothing will be solved here.

Another unique feature of the camogie attire is the name of each player printed on the back of their jersey. It's our signature look, and something that doesn't feature in any other code of gaelic games. In an effort to promote the sport, the Camogie Association first introduced that stylish addition to the jerseys for the 2010 All-Ireland intermediate final between Offaly and Wexford, and the senior decider between Galway and Wexford.

I think it's brilliant for the game to help viewers become familiar with the players on the pitch, particularly if it's their first or second time to watch the sport. Unlike gaelic football, helmets create a barrier in that regard and the names on the back are a great solution to help identify each player on the pitch.

It makes sense to me to bring names on jerseys into all codes of the GAA. We can be more than just a number on a jersey. It brings a bit of individuality to playing gear that is otherwise quite uniform as well. It might be perceived as a feature that's more synonymous with soccer, but so what?

We've borrowed ideas from that sport before and the world didn't implode. As a player, there's some power and ownership in knowing that the shirt is displaying your name on the back.

G. O'CONNOR confirms who I am and that I'm here to work for Cork.

THERE ARE A lot of O'Connors in Cork, and at one stage in my career I shared the half-back line with Mary O'Connor and Paula O'Connor.

Every time we played together, the commentator would say, 'The three O'Connors… no relation'. Cases of mistaken identity were a regular burden for us to live with.

Paula comes from the Newtownshandrum club and is the sister of the famous twin brothers Ben and Jerry. They've lifted the Liam MacCarthy Cup five times between them with Cork and have won one senior All-Ireland title with the club. So people would regularly make the wrong assumption when they see me out and about.

'Are you Ben and Jerry's sister?'

'No, that's Paula!'

*****

WE'RE AT THE Mardyke in the middle of a punishing track session circa 2017, and I'm puffing my last. My long-serving teammate Orla Cotter is running beside me, similarly struggling stride for stride.

We're giving it our all, but we're just not the top dogs anymore. The younger members of the panel, with youth on their side, are accelerating past us. They're looking smaller and smaller as they push on into the distance while Orla and I reach deep into our lungs, coughing and spluttering our way through the laps.

I'm propelling my legs and arms just as hard as everyone else but my engine is carrying more wear and tear. The gap between us just keeps increasing.

These track sessions are pure pre-season work. Putting money in the bank to build up our engines for the season ahead. Perfecting your running technique, injury prevention and putting the ground work in place for your conditioning are the key markers to hit here.

You're getting the body and lungs working.

Once we step out onto the pitch, all the running work is done… with a hurley in my hand and a helmet on my head. That's the way you'll be when you're in a match situation, so it's important to replicate that at training.

A typical night of this pre-season torture consists of 10x100m sprints, 10x50m sprints… with some 200m runs and some 400m runs blended into the mix. They're a terror for players in the peak of their sporting lives, and they get even harder as you get older.

For Orla and myself, two players entering the winter of our careers, these runs are septic.

Circles of hell.

'THIS IS S**T!' Orla manages to blurt out, in between the breaths that are scratching our throats.

Of course, she's right!

This is misery, but I know exactly what to say to her. I've already made peace with our new place in the pack.

'D'YA KNOW… the only way… TO DEAL WITH THIS… ORLA?

'And the only reason… WHY I'M STILL DOING THIS… to just… ACCEPT…

'That you're getting… OLD…

'But still do your best… don't LOOK… AT ANYBODY ELSE…

'Don't… THINK… about… falling behind… THE PACK…

'WORRYING… about getting to certain… TARGETS.

'You have your own… STANDARD for where you are… IN LIFE… AND… once you accept that…

'Things become… A BIT… EASIER!!'

WE'RE JUST IN a different place in our careers now and we must adapt to that. It's not the sound of the death knell or a time for preparing retirement statements, but we can't keep measuring our effort based on what we did before.

When you're younger, you're in your prime.

The targets you set for yourself are easier to achieve when you have an unworn engine. I was very fit in my prime… I was always up at the top of those runs. The pressure was always there to be competitive, and win those runs as often as possible.

If I wasn't in the top three, there was something seriously wrong. That was my benchmark and I never allowed myself any concessions.

The problem with having a driven mindset though is that it stays with you as you age. Your body gradually breaks down but your mind doesn't follow. It stays sharp, hungry and determined. And that's the undoing of an athlete who's getting older.

That mentality is hard to shake.

It's almost as if your brain diverts down two different roads… one takes the logical route, and the other follows the path of a dreamer. Both sides are at war with each other and you have to take action to change your outlook.

If you don't, and you hold onto that youthful mindset as you get older, you're going to suffer desperately. It's not going to happen for you anymore and getting frustrated with that is just seconds wasted.

The dreamer side of your brain is never fully silenced and you'll entertain those delusions from time to time, but learning how to dial it down is enough to keep you on track.

You're not disimproving… you're just getting older.

You're still able to train hard, but you must accept where you are and adjust your expectations.

I have different attributes to give to the game now, compared to what I could give when I was younger. And different doesn't mean less, or worse.

It's obviously tough when you're running around the track and you have people driving past you but, in saying that, there are times when I find myself coming in ahead of some of the young cubs.

Whenever that happens, I'm thinking… *I'm getting past you when you're in your prime?*

Get your ass in gear. That shouldn't be happening.

Being a target for the younger players in these runs is a way for me to reinvent my role in the squad.

✶

I'M PLAYING AN away league club game for the Barr's, around 2017 or '18. Our opponents are a great GAA club with a fine set-up, but today, we've been brought to play this game at a Community School pitch.

Are we really still at this prehistoric stage in gaelic games where a women's game is turfed out to a sub-standard pitch? I'm not at all happy at the sight of this venue.

This just isn't good enough for a senior game. Maybe there was a fixture clash and the main pitch was needed for another game, but that still doesn't justify bringing us here.

I understand that facilities often belong to the men's side of a GAA club, and they're loaned to us when we need them, but this is a senior game that should be played on a pitch that reflects the significance of the match. Our status should be treated with respect, but nothing will improve unless we raise our voices and demand better treatment.

In terms of facilities, the Cork camogie team is treated to the best of the best. Whether it's pre-season, regular season, indoor or outdoor sessions, we always train at top standard facilities. I appreciate that that's not the reality for a lot of teams in women's sports, but we're well looked after here. Even beyond that, my playing experience has been positive.

I've played in very few crap pitches in my time at county level.

But it's the one area where I would have to give credit to the Camogie Association. Whenever we play in Cork, we are never handed anything less than a quality pitch. I've played a good few times in Páirc Uí Chaoimh, and we're always permitted the use of Páirc Uí Rinn whenever we need it.

I've played in some of the best pitches across the country, including Nowlan Park in Kilkenny, and Wexford Park. Perhaps there were one or two league games that were held in a pitch that wasn't quite an inter-county ground, but the venue was still perfectly adequate for our needs.

The Barr's uphold good standards of equality too.

We operate on a one-club policy which ensures equal treatment for all male and female members in the club. The men's football, ladies football, hurling and camogie teams are well catered for. There are three main pitches on the club grounds and all teams are allocated a time slot to ensure that everyone gets an equal amount of access to the facilities.

We all get the opportunity to play on the main pitch for games.

There might be a clash from time to time, but it tends to balance itself out. The third pitch is referred to as the camogie pitch but that's more of a nickname, really. Underage games for the girls and boys teams are usually held on that pitch.

CHAPTER 7

Rena Buckley took a look at Gemma's leg and said it didn't look good. Dr Con said to fear the worst. My brother Kevin is well qualified on the rehab side of things and he agreed that there wasn't a hope. But I would always look at the positive, and if someone was going to make it... it was going to be Gemma.

– Paudie Murray, Cork camogie manager, 2017

IT'S AUGUST 2017 and I get to the B&B in Limerick at about 10pm, where there's a right frosty reception waiting for me at the door.

'I didn't know whether you were coming at all!' the owner says a few minutes later, when she's had a chance to calm down from the fright of a guest arriving this late in the night. I'm genuinely sorry to be checking in at this hour, but right now, I really need to get into my room and get ice on my left knee.

I should really be at home to rehab this injury.

That's what I was warned to do after the game. But I also have a promise to keep to Aoife, who's waiting for me over in the Aran Islands attending a friend's wedding. I've already missed the main event by playing in the All-Ireland semi-final against Galway today, and there'll be murder if I'm not around for the Day 2 celebrations.

I start working on my knee, testing out its limitations.

I can kind of move my ankle up and down, but I can't rotate or swing my knee out left or right. Well, that's definitely not the kind of flexibility you're aiming for with an All-Ireland final coming up in three weeks.

I replay the incident in my head.

I'm standing in the pitch of the Gaelic Grounds in Limerick, watching the play unfold in the second-half. I'm in the ready position, which, in hurling speak, means that I'm holding my hurley horizontally with one hand on either side of the stick. It's hurling 101 for any player starting out in the game.

You must be in the ready position anytime you're not directly involved in the game. My two legs are pointing forward and the play is now coming towards me. But I'm not mobile and I can't explain why.

Now, I can see my teammate Ashling Thompson is fighting for the ball with Galway's Aoife Donohue. Amidst the pushing and shoving, they fall… and the weight of their momentum shoots straight into the side of my knee.

A POPPING sound immediately follows.

I'm down on the ground, needing treatment.

We're deep into the second-half and the game is delicately balanced. I try to play on, hoping that my knee is just feeling a bit weak after the bang. But I feel all the power drain out as I try to run. Carrying on like this would compromise the team, so I surrender to the pain and ask to be taken off.

WE HOLD ON for a three-point win.

After stretching our lead to eight points at the start of the second-half, we then went almost half an hour without a score as Galway came roaring back at us with a late flourish. But we get over the line to reach our fourth All-Ireland final in-a-row.

It's instant elation at the thought of getting back to Croke Park, but that feeling soon gives way to panic as the sound of my knee going off like a firework starts rushing back. *Feck, we're in a final!* My teammate Rena Buckley is a physio and she takes a look at it when we get back into the dressing-room.

I get back on the team bus and take my seat.

I'm staring at my knee and trying to assess where to go from here when Aoife Murray comes down for a chat.

'Look!' she begins, 'We'll just get on with it. We'll deal with it.'

'Yeah, yeah... we'll deal with it...,' I agree.

I won't get an Oscar for that performance and Aoife can probably tell as she diverts the conversation away to anything but the obvious. We review the game and start talking about the final, and everything outside the injury, before pulling into the Woodlands Hotel in Limerick, where I part ways with the team.

It's probably better this way that I have somewhere else to be, instead of being around the team for the evening and having the same conversation over and over again about something that I don't have any answers for.

I was in bother today when it happened, and I'm in an even bigger spot now in the B&B, trying to plan how I'm going to get my knee investigated while also keeping my word to Aoife. I know I must prioritise my knee but I can't let her down.

I wanted to be here at the B&B earlier, but we were delayed at the stadium after the game. Some girls were required for drug-testing and one of them was too dehydrated to go to the toilet. The delay in waiting for her to provide a sample meant we didn't leave the stadium until late in the evening.

I get onto a friend and she tells me that if I go to the Galway clinic, I can get an MRI scan... and get the results there and then. Aoife and I are already booked into the G Hotel to stretch out the wedding into a few days of a break for us, so now... I have a plan.

Wedding first... and MRI after to determine the damage.

ONCE I GET the news, I get straight onto the famous Dr Con Murphy. He's not part of the Cork camogie backroom team, but he is the number one person to call for any medical-related issue in our county. An elite GAA physician.

He organises my physio work with fellow Cork man Colin Lane. While all that is falling into place, I start hatching another plan. I get an ice machine and put the cubes on my knee two to three times a day. My aim is to get through this by degrees.

Baby steps. Tiny little movements, tiny little jumps... running in straight lines, and plenty of clean eating. I need to go to Páirc Uí Rinn and to my own club in St Finbarr's to get more work done there too. That's all I can do to give myself the best opportunity of being fit for the All-Ireland final against Kilkenny.

Paudie doesn't really have a hands-on role in my rehab and just leaves me to work away with Colin and Liam O'Reilly, who is our S&C coach. Eager to stop the girls from getting distracted by my progress, Paudie advises me to stay away from the group for now and rehab alone. Paudie is never too far away though. He checks in whenever he gets word that I might be losing hope.

'I don't know if you're going to be able to play.'

That's what the doctor said to me when he explained that my MRI scan revealed a grade two MCL tear. Crucially, that term doesn't start with the letter 'A' which stands for anterior. An ACL tear would not be a conquerable injury in this amount of time. That's a minimum of six months out of action. That would end my season.

I'm fortunate on that score, but it's still a rotten injury to get this close to the final. A six-week timeframe for a full recovery is what I'm told, and I only have three weeks and a day from when it happened in the semi-final. So, that's crap.

News of my impending absence hits the public and there's a bit of confusion as some people think that it was an ankle injury that forced me off against Galway. It's true that I did previously have a problem with my ankle, but this is a separate issue entirely. That's more of a sidebar though.

The main headline revolves around my availability for the final. And the word from our camp is that I won't be fit to play. That's the official medical opinion on the matter, so we have to follow that for now. And honestly, I don't really know what I will or won't be fit for on September 10, when the curtain is pulled up in Croke Park for the All-Ireland final. Management pass on the same message to the team.

As far as the players are aware, I'm out. That might be disappointing news for them to hear, but ruling me out of selection early on is the best way to handle it. It's the most definitive answer to give and removes all doubt. My teammates don't have to worry about what I'm doing if they believe that I'm not physically fit to do anything. They'll have a clearer head to focus all of their energy on the game.

No doubt people are asking them questions about me too, and if my teammates have no insight about my recovery plan, then they don't have any secrets to keep when people come looking for an answer.

'Is Gemma playing?'

'Is Gemma not playing?'

All they have to say is, 'No, she's out… she's not training with us.'

It cuts off the line of inquiry straightaway and takes all the pressure off the players. Those conversations are probably not so straightforward in Kilkenny households. They don't know anything concrete, so their players can't give any concrete answers. My situation is still the same the week leading up to the final.

I'm unfit to play is still the official party line when the team is announced on the Friday before the game. Paudie rejigs the team to name Meabh Cahalane at wing-back, while Ashling Thompson is moving into my spot at centre-back. Paudie is a mind games specialist and he wants to push my injury status to at least create some uncertainty in the Kilkenny squad.

I'm aware of the media attention and I see one or two of the reports, but I have to zone out from all the noise.

IT'S THE THURSDAY night before the final and I've just received a text. It's Aoife Murray testing the waters after my first training session with the group since injuring my knee.

'Well, how did you get on?'

'Not too bad at all. I didn't want the training to end.'

IT'S THE EVE of the All-Ireland final and myself and Aoife Murray are in our room at the Crown Plaza Hotel. The team travelled up by train, as they traditionally do, but I came up to Dublin by car with Aoife because I had to drop my bags off in McKee Barracks, as I am starting a course in UCD on the Monday after the All-Ireland. When I mentioned this to Paudie, he was delighted... he didn't want all the prematch talk amongst the girls to be about my knee. I suppose he's protecting the girls from fixating on my fitness for the game, and this allows me to squeeze every spare second into my recovery.

But now we're all assembled in the hotel and getting ready to kip down for the night. Aoife and I have just returned from a team meeting to see that our glasses of wine have arrived. The glass of wine we always share the night before an All-Ireland final.

A nightcap is particularly needed right now with all the stress involved in the preparation for tomorrow. I start to slip into my compression ice machine, which Colin Lane gave to me to assist with accelerating the rehab. It's basically a box that folds over and creates cold air around the knee. I bring it everywhere with me and had it on while we were down in Rossmore recently for our usual pre-final bonding camp.

Aoife was rooming with me again for that trip and when she pulled back the curtains the morning after we arrived, we discovered that our room was facing out onto a graveyard. We could only laugh at that ominous sight, hoping that we weren't cursed.

We're sipping on our wine tonight and trying to wind down as Aoife ices her knee after taking a knock during the week. Both in the wars, albeit to varying degrees of a battle. We both look at each other, thinking, *What are we at?*

Anyone else would call us lunatics for this carry-on.

All you can do is laugh at the insanity of it all. There's a noise at the door that's somehow unlocked, and suddenly some faces appear from the corridor. And then some more pile in. The secret Wine Supper Summit has been exposed. *Caught rotten!*

The craic and the chats kick off instantly with the players and management who have called in. Some of the stories are hilarious and, already, my mood is improving.

I've reached acceptance with my situation… either this plan will work or it won't. Either my knee will co-operate for the hour or it will buckle like blocks of Jenga.

*****

UNDER PAUDIE, NOTHING is a drill at training.

That 'D' word is outlawed here. Everything we do is purposeful, and oriented towards what we do in a match. His brother Kevin is our trainer and his aim is to turn us into problem solvers and decision-makers on the pitch. And to show some invention while we do it.

Of course, the trainings are intense too, but how we think is a major cornerstone of our success. It's baked right into our mindset for the 2017 and '18 seasons.

If you're trying to move from A to B to C, you don't necessarily have to go through station B in order to get to C. There's no rule that says you must go through every point alphabetically. You can go directly to the end point.

Kevin doesn't want us to think like robots. Growing up, I think maybe people are prevented from thinking for themselves as athletes. Kevin's training is a little bit different in terms of the way he thinks about the game. He empowers us to come up with our own solutions for every different set of problems that a game presents.

That's why the concept of a drill is worthless here.

Every activity at training must be tailored to a match-like situation. You might start off doing something with one or two cones there but, eventually, he takes away the cones and the monotony of our movement. Going from A to B is a linear way of thinking and if you're too reliant on that style of training, you should just lift your brain out of your head and put it to one side while you go through the motions.

So, once you take away the cones and the predictability out of the training session, there could be four or five balls involved and people moving in different directions. That's far more stimulating.

It just gets people thinking and exercises like that help elevate the leaders and more vocal players to the forefront of the group. It also shows the players who might be fading into the background because they don't know what's going on. It's okay not to know what's going on because I often feel like that at training. I might be looking around, wondering what's happening, but I don't stay confused for long.

I'm not afraid to speak up and ask for direction, whereas others just go through it and they mightn't know because they don't want to ask why we're doing this. It's vital to be vocal, to have good channels of communication within the team, and to have accountability. You learn so much about yourself and your teammates through training like this, and people probably don't even realise that until they reflect on it.

And when you practice that concept of taking ownership of your place in the team, you can bring it into match situations.

*****

IT'S HALF-TIME IN the 2008 All-Ireland final, and Aoife Murray is addressing the group to apologise for a mistake she made. Three minutes before the break, she conceded a goal after dropping a ball over her head.

A high ball coming in like that is normally a bread and butter job for Aoife, but she just misread the flight on this occasion and the ball slipped through her grasp. Aoife is obviously an excellent goalkeeper, but at the same time, she made a mistake and if she feels that the goal was solely her mistake, she always puts her hand up to say she's sorry. That kind of selfless act is not uncommon for her.

Of course, we always reassure her that we're *all* responsible for any costly errors. And if an opposition player slips through and it's one-on-one, then that's not the goalkeeper's fault. We, as outfield players, are Aoife's protectors and we should never expose her to that kind of danger.

In a situation like that, everything favours the forward and Aoife's chances of saving the impending shot are probably less than 50 percent. If the ball bounces and trickles past her, then that's human error, and we're all guilty of those mistakes. Every player has their skid marks.

The only difference is the extent of the consequences when those errors happen. If a defender makes a mistake, it puts us under pressure and there's a possibility of the opposition getting a score. But depending on the severity of the mistake and its location on the pitch, we might still be able to recover in time to avert the danger. If Aoife makes a mistake, there's no safety net for her.

A goal for the other team is always the price she'll have to pay. That's the dreadful trade-off for a goalkeeper.

Transparency is everything for a team that wants to achieve great things together. Aoife doesn't hide from what happened before half-time, and we already know that she has the resilience to charge on again. She's rewarded for her willingness to be accountable in the second-half as she pulls off three super saves.

The first comes just five minutes after the restart when she saves a penalty from Jessica Gill. Aoife comes to our rescue twice more before the end of the game, to help us to a five-point victory. Galway could have completely altered the trajectory of the game had they converted even one of those chances.

We all make mistakes but it's about having the confidence to get on with it, and know that you can park that mistake and reset. Aoife's actions in the second-half is an excellent demonstration of that. And if it's me that messes up, I'll do something in the next play to get myself back on track. I'll ensure that my player doesn't get the ball the next time, or I'll get a pass into the forwards, or I'll get a hook in.

You can always mess up, but it's vital not to let that moment overwhelm you or make you think that your game is over. You can still feel confident that you'll get it right the next time and not crumble into yourself. We're lucky to have players with that kind of strong-willed personality in the Cork squad.

It's one of the features that gives us the edge over other teams.

Our team meetings are conducted in a similarly honest and frank fashion. Instead of just firing out buzz words and saying what we already know about the job at hand, our discussions are game-focused. Paudie and Kevin go through scenarios in a game and ask players what our next move should be in that sequence.

We bring notepads and iPads with us for those meetings and jot down the important points of information. I don't tend to write too much though, and just take note of anything new that I need to remember. A lot of the stuff that comes up already makes sense to me but there's still loads for me to learn in these sessions. Activities like this get people thinking and encourage them to apply what we do at training to a match situation. It keeps the brain sharp and active, always ready to respond to unexpected events in a game.

Matches at county level entail so much more than just lining out and playing away. You can't predict all the scenarios that will test your reactions, but you must be prepared to try and handle them the best way you can. These mental exercises prompt people to think for themselves and engage in problem-solving. You can put a game plan in place but it's never going to materialise the way you want it to.

Nine times out of 10, the plan can only be executed so far and other things will happen to push the plan out of shape. It's up to the players then to react to what's happening and solve the issues as they arise.

When a game is in the melting point, that philosophy which Paudie, Kevin and the rest of the backroom team has imparted to us is what pushes us over the line. Our set-up is just so well arranged and we really reap the benefits of those sessions. Our in-house matches follow the same kind of line.

Paudie would probably bring in a referee who might intentionally officiate the games badly to test us. To keep the numbers even, he sometimes brings in players from the minor or intermediate squads. For other games, we might play against a boys' underage team to up the physicality stakes and put some iron in our chests for the big games coming down the line. Those games can be a great self-esteem booster for us when the lads start underestimating what's ahead of them.

They come strolling onto the pitch, throwing shapes and expecting to do nothing more than some showboating to get the better of us. We crash straight into them from the throw-in and they quickly realise that they're in a game with us. That sets them off into turning on each other before eventually copping on and giving us a proper game of hurling.

I've always known that boys can be tricky to play against. I've shared a pitch with them ever since I was young. Some of them just aren't comfortable with the idea of a girl being their equal on the pitch. They're developing hormones and just feeling insecure about their manhood being threatened.

They make assumptions about me that they will later regret. 'Oh yes there's a girl on their team.' Big mistake, pal!

Once we start playing, I give them a right land with what I can do when there's a ball at my feet or a hurley in my hand. They start getting cranky and narky, but I'm happy to help them learn and grow.

CHAPTER 8

I'M AROUND EIGHT or nine, and mam and I are heading down the road to a place called Coláiste Stiofáin Naofa. It's a technical college in Ballyphehane and it's our special spot. We're not here to enrol in any classes though… we're here for a puck, a scream, a cry… and a fling of the hurley on the big pitch outside.

We're here every Friday and Saturday for all of that.

There are some big fields here that we call poppy fields. It's my favourite playground and I could spend hours here. We practice everything… frees, catching balls overhead… striking off the left, striking off the right… running onto the ball, and hitting it from a standing position.

Mam and I cover every base. She's trying to teach me to be as adaptable and versatile as I can be and I'm fully here for all of it. I'm a sponge for every word she says. That quality has to be in your DNA if you want to prosper in sport. There's only so much you can teach when a child is starting out… they need to soak up the instruction and practice relentlessly.

You either have that hunger or you don't.

Some kids don't have the interest no matter how much you try to nurture their talent. You could be saying all the right things but if they don't want to receive it, it just goes in one ear and out the other. Of course, you can play for the enjoyment, and the fun of it. That's how it should be. It's important to strike the appropriate balance between motivation and smothering a child.

You want to encourage them to be great, not drill the hurling out of them by being too strict. Parents living vicariously through their children's talent isn't good either, especially if it's not what their child wants. That just leads them down a road that ends in resentment towards the sport. But at the same time, kids can be very competitive too.

Mam knows how to nurture that with me.

Everyday we're here, I'm giving mam my full attention as she teaches me the importance of knowing that it's not enough to just have a talent for hitting a ball with the hurley. You have to work hard for it. I obviously have my own drive but she enhances it. Dad gets involved as well. He's a massive GAA fan and he often pucks the ball around with us out the back of the house.

He plays his part, even if we start laughing at him when he mishits the sliotar. But mam is just so invested in it. She's my driving force and my inspiration. I have a lot of friends whose parents take an interest in their kids' training, but I don't think any of them could match my mam's effort. Everything starts from her.

My ground zero.

Stiofáin Naofa is a great spot to do a bit of messing with your friends too. There's a security guard who works here at night and we like to have a bit of fun with him when it's time to lock up. Basically, we're just trying to stay in here for as long as possible without getting caught.

So, when he gets the torch out, we sneak into the bushes and see how long we can last before he catches us. It's mainly me and my friends who hang around Stiofáin Naofa, but you get some passing groups of older people here too. Sometimes they're out drinking and they might call over to us every now and then. But they don't really bother us or try to interfere.

Nothing disturbs the peace when we're out here having the craic in these parks.

I COME FROM a strong hurling bloodline.

Mam comes from the parish of Faranree which is where Na Piarsaigh GAA club can be found. Mam and my mam's family always supported Glen Rovers, which is in the parish of Blackpool. Most families in Faranree would support the parish club, but my mam's family were one of the few who supported the Glen.

Mam's brother Bill captained the Cork minors to an All-Ireland in 1974, and it was through Bill that mam developed an interest in the sport. She played soccer before that, but once she discovered The Glen, she was hooked on hurling and camogie. She just loved it from the start.

She loves the club so much that she actually named her son after Glen Rovers. They won the Cork county championship in 1989, which was the same year that Glenn was born. Glenn for Glen. My dad had other names in mind (Finbarr was probably among them) but mam got her way in the end. It's a strange sound to hear… 'Come on, Glenn O'Connor " whenever he's playing for the Barr's in a match against Glen Rovers.

Mam gave up camogie early on and she always regretted it. She played with the likes of Mary Newman, a stalwart of Cork camogie, and they became quite friendly. Maybe it was due to work or lifestyle choices that mam decided to leave it, but she still has a passion for the sport. She's passing the torch to me now and the flame is still strong as it burns through me.

Mam is with me at every stage of my playing career. She's even there for the important moments when I can't be.

It's 2004 and I'm on a tour of duty with the Irish Defence Forces in Liberia. I miss out on the first-ever camogie All Star awards ceremony at home as a result, but mam is there. She collects the award on my behalf, and I'm happy knowing that the trophy is in her safe hands. She's the only person I want to pick it up for me.

The award eventually makes its way out to me in Liberia, and it's in the possession of a very special dignitary, President Mary McAleese. She's here to visit the troops just before Christmas, and during her trip she makes the presentation to me. I miss out on the 2009 All Star awards again while on tour in Chad, but mam has my back again to deputise when my name is called during the ceremony.

It's a nice way for her to get some recognition too for her contribution to my career, and to the sport of camogie.

*****

MY FIRST HURLEY comes in a plastic bag. I take it out, look at the red tape on it, admire the shape of it and start practicing my swing straightaway. I can already feel it becoming an extension of me. My third arm.

The first flashes of playing for Cork start running through my mind. My head is bursting with possibilities. I'm blessed that sport comes naturally to me and

I'm able to hit the ball from the first strike. The sweet connection between bás and sliotar clicks in right there from the start. That willingness to learn and put coaching into practice starts in school for me, and I'm ready to make my mark now, in fifth class, in the famous Sciath na Scol competition. For any youngster growing up in Cork, this is serious business.

It's the first real taste of competitive games for young kids. Mam is by my side for all of it, having a chat and motivating me before the matches. She does that for the other kids too, and the ones who really want to learn know it's in their best interest to absorb her words of encouragement. I know this is only a primary school competition but if it's there to be won, well... I want to win it. And we do.

We're in Páirc Uí Rinn and the heavens are opening up to let the rain lash down on us. We win by 10-0 to 3-0. No points. Goals only. The scoreline reads more like what you see at a soccer match, but I don't care.

This is the best day ever.

It's the first step in my development as a hurler. The first major box to be ticked and my first bit of silverware. We head back to school for the winner's banquet at the chipper.

A feast of chips and sausages for the champions.

The first spoils of war.

Now I'm really starting to visualise a path that leads to putting on a Cork jersey. I pass some familiar faces on that road. A girl called Jenny O'Leary, who is a year or two older than me, keeps coming up as an opponent. Later on, I come across someone else called Jacqui Hurley during trials for Cork. Aoife Murray is there too.

There's a circle of us playing together from under-14 to under-16. We have city division competitions and hurling street leagues in Cork. Our team wins a few and loses a few of these. All part of growing up and learning to deal with victory and defeat. I win the Féile individual skills competition at 13 in Cork, which means I get to progress to the All-Ireland stage as my county's representative.

But I end up tanking the job when I head up to Enniscorthy in Wexford for my big moment. Normally, I can perform these skills with my eyes closed, but today is an absolute nightmare for me. Fundamentals like mishitting the ball are tripping me up.

Everyday can't be your day!

MY FIRST BIG chance to wear the red of Cork comes via those Primary Schools games. With those games in Cork, there's a selection process involved where players are handpicked to play at half-time when the county's hurlers are in action. It all depends on the hurlers of course, and how long they last in the championship. By the time I'm chosen to play at half-time, Cork get knocked out. And we're in an era where the GAA championships are straight knockout competitions, so there are no second chances. Just my luck! There goes my first opportunity to represent Cork.

I finally get my turn through a Cork under-14 competition, but this time, I'll be playing a few exhibition matches before the senior camogie games. The gear doesn't really fit because I'm still really small and skinny. The jersey drops down around my ankles like a night dress. I'm drowning in red.

The skorts have to be pinned back on us and they're pleated too. One drop of rain and you feel like you're carrying a cement block around your waist.

I've been hearing about Cork camogie since I first held that plastic hurley. I've been to one or two of their finals too, looking at the team that I hope to one day play for. Of course, I'm aware of the Cork hurlers too and indeed all the successes that both teams have brought home to Leeside.

The St Finbarr's club in Togher is my home club, but it's in Ballyphehane that I first learned to puck the ball. Ballyphehane is my home parish and the club grounds are right around the corner from my house. Our area of Cork city includes suburbs like Togher, Turner's Cross – where Cork City football club play their home games – and the Lough. It's a nice sizable catchment area.

Geographically, it makes sense for me to play for Ballyphehane and I've enjoyed my formative years here learning all the elements of the game. However, it just doesn't match the stature of the Barr's, and if I want to take my game further and realise my dreams with Cork, this can't be my club forever.

I'm nine years old and I'm starting to come to terms with this hard truth.

I considered playing for my mam's club in Glen Rovers and we did road test the idea when she drove me over there to attend a training session. We tried it for a fit, but it didn't work out. It was a nightmare trying to make it across the city from Ballyphehane and we were sitting in traffic for about 50 minutes. That's a punishing commute, and nine is a bit young to be even trying to commit to something like that every week.

To the Barr's it is so.

Again, mam is by my side when I arrive at the club for my first-ever training session. Marian McCarthy, who is a stalwart of the club and a former player with the Barr's, is there to greet us on my first day and welcome me as their new recruit.

My switch from Ballyphehane to the Barr's is the only answer if you're serious about progressing in the sport. It's similar to the move Roy Keane made when he was starting out as a soccer player in Cork. Roy was born in Mayfield, which is on the northside of Cork city. But as his soccer aspirations began to bloom, he knew he needed to move on. He was around nine too when he chose to play for Rockmount, a club which was better equipped to nurture his burgeoning talent.

Sometimes you have to make difficult decisions to give yourself the best chance of succeeding in sport, and switching to the Barr's is a natural progression for some people in the Ballyphehane club, though others still choose to stick with their parish club. It's the same for my brother Glenn and many other young players from the area.

IN CORK, OUR under-16 grade is classed as minor. And succeeding at minor is of life or death importance. Another stepping stone. It's my first proper introduction to county camogie where we're out training three times a week and there's a lot of serious running in the sessions. Before getting to that stage, we go for trials in Ballygarvan to see who cuts the mustard.

There's 50 or 60 of us here, all auditioning for the honour of playing for Cork. This is where I run into Jacqui Hurley, years before she becomes a famous sports presenter for RTÉ. Future goalkeeping great Aoife Murray is there too. The trials last for a few weeks, so you know they're being thorough about who they select for the squad. There's such a conveyor belt of players being swapped in and out during the trial games and you might only get one or two opportunities.

That's what makes managers at underage level so important because it's about identifying these little things and seeing those attributes in players. They're assessing you on your ability to contribute to team play, as well as your athleticism. It's not all about the cut and dry of turning a ball over and scoring. Mam and her twin sister come with us to watch.

Afterwards, I ask my mam for a review of my performance at corner-forward. I'm not convinced by how I played.

'I wasn't really on the ball a lot,' I say to her.

'Look, what harm if it doesn't work out? You're only 13!' she replies.

I rush to my mam after every game to get her thoughts. I don't care what anyone else thinks. I could get Player of the Match, and a back slap from every single person there. The President of Ireland could call to give me a personal congratulations on a job well done, and it wouldn't register. My mam's opinion is the only one that matters to me.

Her approval is all I hear. If she doesn't tell me that I had a good game, well then... it's settled. Let the records show that I was sh** today. She's not a pushy parent but she is honest with me. And she has her little phrases that let you know what she thought of my performance.

Little tells to cushion the blow of a negative review.

'Jesus, you'd a great game today, girl. You were awesome.' That one is fairly straightforward and it's all I need to hear to reassure me that I was on form.

The exchange after a bad day at the office goes a bit differently. I know she wasn't impressed when she goes quiet.

'What did you think of the game?'

'Yeah. You could be moving a lot better. You look a bit tired.'

I might argue my case from time to time, but nine times out of 10, she's bang on in her assessment. She gives me unvarnished honesty because she wants me to do my best, and she knows there's better in me. She's a crazy supporter on the sidelines at matches. Not to an abusive extent, but she's very vocal.

I get a warm feeling when I hear her voice come roaring out onto the pitch. She argues our corner when decisions don't go our way and she's right in the pocket with every ruck and tackle. She has her socks rolled up over whatever tracksuit she's wearing.

'GO ON... GIVE IT TO EM, GIRL!' she screams out.

She does get quite animated but you want her on your sideline. I can hear my Dad's voice booming up from the bank too. My family come to every game.

There's always the same families and the same faces at our matches. It's a small number but it creates a tight-knit community of support for us and everyone gets to know each other quite intimately. It's a common sight in women's sport. When you stop playing, you're almost taking that opportunity away from your family because they step away from the team with you.

It's not that you have to stop attending the games when your girl retires, but it's less common to go to the games when you're not directly connected to someone that's involved in the squad. The fan base isn't as wide and neutral as what you see in the men's game. It's a pity, but it's also probably a reflection of where camogie is at in terms of development.

There's still a long road to go to grow the game.

✱

THE RESULTS ARE in from the Cork minor trials that I went to. They obviously saw something in me, because I've been called back in and I've made the cut. John Cronin, from the Cloughduv club, is our manager.

What? I'm really in?

It's just so exciting to hear that he wants to take a punt on me when I've barely entered my teenage years. John's training is gruelling. His daughter Ciara conducts the running training with us and she torments us with full throttle sprints the diagonal length of a pitch. We know what's coming when we see her rocking up to our sessions.

That kind of structured training environment delivers two All-Ireland titles for this Cork squad – one against Galway in 1999 when I'm still 13, and another against Kilkenny in 2001.

Pa Finn is the manager when I first get called into the Cork seniors in 2002. He's a hurling fanatic and a great Barr's man with a great knowledge of the game. He might not have an equal insight into the camogie scene in Cork but he has a brilliant brain for this sport. Our training base is at the Mardyke in UCC and I'm so eager to impress.

I'm 17, and sharing a dressing-room with some of Cork's finest camogie products. The room is crammed with proven winners... Linda Mellerick, Denise Cronin, Mary O'Connor, Vivienne Harris, Fiona O'Driscoll, Eithne Duggan, Stephanie Dunlea... they're all here.

These are players that I have idolised from a young age, and now I have been deemed worthy of a spot on the same team as them. Fiona O'Driscoll might be small in stature but she always gives an honest effort. Linda Mellerick would happily throw her head in front of a moving truck to get the ball. This is a group that is ravenous for success.

They're hardy too. Smashed teeth and busted lips in every corner of the dressing-room. It's like a crime scene here after matches. Carnage.

Wearing a helmet is not compulsory and this team definitely got that memo. These players will gallop straight into a wall of gunfire. We're in an era that predates drinking bans and the widely accepted health advice is to enjoy a few bottles in conjunction with the hard graft. These girls love their few drinks and they're not criminals for being that way.

They train hard, they want to win, but they're not enslaved by the sport either. After games, we often stop off at an off licence and buy a box of bottles. We have the craic, go to the pub and have a few drinks. We blow off a little bit of steam after each game, and keep everything in moderation, rather than staying off booze entirely for the whole season only to go feral when we get released back into the wild in the off-season.

The great Sandie Fitzgibbon, a six-time All-Ireland winner with Cork, is part of the management team. I'm getting hard imposter syndrome as we head out to play. *Wow, what's happening?* I just want to give my best and prove my value here. Yes, there's an expectation to live up to, but the nerves don't pile up too much on me.

I feel carefree and I have nothing to lose.

IT'S MY DEBUT season and we finish the year as All-Ireland champions, beating Tipperary by 4-9 to 1-9 in Croke Park. Achieving this alongside players that I've looked up to ever since I was first presented with that plastic hurley is pretty special. A real eye-opener to how winning on the biggest stage of all can make you feel.

This is what hard work, backboned by talent, can produce.

The Gospel according to my mam.

CHAPTER 9

IT'S 2004 AND GUNSHOTS are ringing out while I'm on a peacekeeping tour of duty in Liberia. We're going into a plantation which has lots of oil and natural minerals. They're rich in iron ore and rubber. Some of the local militia are trying to take over the plantation and that puts us in a vulnerable position.

We soon receive our orders that we're going in, as the sound of gunfire starts to rumble from next door.

It takes just seconds for everything to change out here.

Conflict is never far away and you must be prepared for anything. Incidents like this one really hammer home the reality that violence can actually kick off when you go overseas. There is risk to life involved in every deployment. Irish soldiers have died on peace-keeping missions.

We're lucky on this occasion though, as tensions are de-escalated and we avoid a possible combat situation. But the threat is always in the air and we end up being on patrol here for eight days. Working in these conditions might sound exciting to someone who seeks adventure, but there's nothing glorious about any of this. We're not here to look for chaos.

We don't take sides in whatever war that has left this land suffering from division, and we never underestimate the volatility of the area.

I never joined the army in the hope of ever ending up in a war zone. I'm certainly not here to go home a hero. You don't join the Defence Forces because you want to go to war, you go because it offers something different for the recruits. It stands for a core set of values that you're interested in and that resonate with you.

You represent the uniform and you're given the opportunity to travel abroad. You also have the honour of representing Ireland, a country that has massive international recognition for peacekeeping.

The glorified image of war in Hollywood movies doesn't help with some of the misunderstanding about what we're here to do. I definitely don't want to go to war because we're already in a world of hurt. The ongoing Russian invasion of Ukraine is such a tragic example of modern warfare.

Why would I want to add to that or be involved in that?

There have been incidents on peacekeeping missions where people have gone overseas and have come close to combat situations. That's why you have to be vigilant and believe in what you're doing, because if something does happen, you have to know what to do and be equipped to react. This incident in Liberia is my close encounter.

The humidity here is ferocious too. The wind doesn't blow, it sucks.

We get special clothes to help us cope with the heat. To keep our temperatures down, we're given tropical pants, which is a light uniform, and a dryflo t-shirt along with socks and boots. While on patrol, you put on the shirt and wear all the other gear. Some troops have air fans in their rooms, which are six-man tents, but there's no air conditioning around here.

Our clothes are constantly soaked in sweat.

There's nothing Hollywood about some of the troubling sights that you see here on duty either. The images that stay that are burned into your brain. During another tour, I'm in the city of Tyre, which is a coastal spot about 45 minutes from Beirut in Lebanon. There's a woman at the side of the road who looks to be in her seventies or eighties.

She has this plastic beach chair with her and she's using it as a zimmer frame. That's not even a basic standard of living. What makes it even worse is that there are very wealthy people here living alongside people who have nothing. Two sets of people from utterly different worlds of social status somehow living side by side.

You understand the importance of this job after seeing people begging on the streets with really bad disabilities and no real appropriate medical supplies to help them live with their condition. There's a massive economic crisis in this part of the world, and it has worsened over the years. The diesel shortage situation is huge and there's a lot of general unrest.

Everything affects everything that happens over here and that causes tension between Israel, South Lebanon, and everything that goes on in the Gaza Strip. The Irish army has a good relationship with the Lebanese, and that's why we're always asked to stay here. But the older generation is petering out and the younger people in the new generation don't really have the respect for the United Nations soldiers here.

They have their own agenda. In an effort to diffuse that tension, our commander will talk to the local mayors in the villages to try and stamp that out.

YOU'RE ALWAYS AWARE of the potential dangers.

Always.

Prior to travelling, each soldier must complete pre-deployment training and a mission readiness exercise. This involves live firing shoots, and a battle inoculation with live rounds of big and small arms firing overhead. This is conducted at a form-up, where the battalion comes together to prepare for the mission before flying out. Overall, I suppose you just go with the current climate.

Coming out to Liberia, we didn't know much more about the mission other than the fact that it was a peace enforcement trip. That means that it's a bit more aggressive and we have a bit more freedom, and we are guided by more robust rules of engagement.

So, I suppose you do worry about those things but you can't stress too much about what could happen... better to just focus on the purpose of your deployment.

I'm not here to be a war veteran or a martyr.

I'm in the Defence Forces for a life of teamwork, camaraderie, the outdoor life and everything else that goes with it. Our peacekeeping missions abroad are exactly that. We're here to coordinate with the United Nations (UN) and keep the peace in a place that's been ripped apart by conflict.

*****

THESE DAYS, I work for the medical corps of the army but I've moved through different posts in my career. My first job was with the fourth infantry battalion in Collins Barracks in Cork. I requested to be stationed with the military police to give me some exposure to life as a guard and keep in touch with the other profession that I had in mind. But I was refused.

'No, you play sport,' I was told. 'You're going to the fourth battalion.'

I spent a lot of years in that unit until a re-organisation in the Defence Forces resulted in the closure of a lot of barracks, including our fourth battalion in 2012. Times were still tough in the aftermath of the economic downturn. The dying embers of the post-recession years still had a bit of a kick in them.

We were surprised by that move because Collins Barracks was a big operation for the southern command at the time, for anything in relation to gardai and Civil Aid assistance. I don't really know what the reason was behind it but that was the decision, and we all got scattered elsewhere. A lot of people got posted to Limerick to the next infantry operational unit, but I was sent to the brigade training centre which is the training school in Cork. I went overseas and came back and spent five years in the brigade training school, where I was able to train the recruits.

The end of your recruitment training is referred to as passing out, where there's a lot of focus on field and tactics. You start putting your training into real life exercises. Another two months. Another tough slog.

Then you move into your respective corp. There's lots of different corps to put your skill-sets to good use. You could be an infantry soldier which is basically a foot soldier. On the ground, there's the artillery, which is operating all the big heavy weapons. Cavalry is all the armoured vehicles.

Then there's the CIS (Communication and Information Services) , where you work with radio and communications. There's also the medical corp, where you do all your medical courses. That's where the bus stops for me because I needed a change.

I ENROL IN a military and medical course in UCD. It's a year-long course and I'm staying in McKee Barracks in Cabra while I head over to Donnybrook to attend the classes. I don't know what it means just yet but it has opened up other possibilities for me. It could lead me down a few different avenues, from joining the National Ambulance Service to maybe considering going down the pre-hospital route.

I don't know about pursuing something like medicine. That's not where I'm at or something I'd be driven to do. But we do a lot of things at work that relate to pre-hospital and occupational medicine. We deal with a lot of injury-based things like knees and ankles, which could possibly bring me down the physical therapy route.

It's definitely something that has opened up my mind to a new world of professional options.

CHAPTER 10

AOIFE MURRAY AND I are a pair in almost every conceivable way. We room together, and we sit side by side in the dressing-room.

And we like our glass of wine the night before the biggest game of the year.

Of course, modern GAA players have to live with a clean diet, but one glass of wine is not going to erase all the good nutrition that you have already banked. It certainly hasn't hindered us from winning 18 All-Ireland medals between us. We're not ritualistic about it.

We don't go to the same bar and sit in the same seats facing east or anything like that. There's no superstition involved... just a glass or two to relax the mind and help us get a better night's sleep. We wouldn't even go and sit in the bar because that would look a bit too casual. A scene like that might suggest that we're going to strike up a few cigarettes and settle in for a night on the high stool.

My diet is naturally good, and I'm quite strict about what I put in my body. I'm not much of a chocolate fiend and I find it pretty easy to keep away from rubbish. Everything for me is savoury and I put more of a focus on portion control with the foods that I do eat. I have a healthy relationship with drink too, and I know how to keep everything in proportion.

I don't agree with the concept of the drinking ban. I think it's a needless rule that doesn't actually achieve what it's intended for. I'm not suggesting that players should be permitted to drink seven nights a week, but it's also safe for a team to sit down together after a game and enjoy a few drinks.

Premier League players do it. Rugby players do it as well, and they're out every week playing games at an intense, professional level of sport. Drinking bans are just a reflection of this silly mentality that the GAA has developed towards alcohol. And it just leads to ridiculous outcomes where players are living like monks and not touching a drink for months and then, as soon as their season ends, they go out and get bananas after a few jars. It's a complete binge drinking culture.

Drinking bans just make alcohol seem more appealing to players. It might not even be about the desire to have a drink, and more about the temptation to be a rule-breaker and to rebel against a regime. To be seen to create a bit of drama.

We're not children who need to be disciplined, though. We're all adults who know the consequences of drinking to excess while trying to be an elite athlete. Removing the prohibition element of the whole thing gives players the freedom to choose how much they want to dedicate themselves to this project. It also establishes a trust between players and management.

You either want to make smart decisions that are in the best interests of the team, or you want to abuse the freedom and get trashed. And if you go with the latter, you probably won't last long in the sport at the top level.

There was a period where things were messy in the Cork squad after All-Ireland finals. The hotel rooms wouldn't get smashed but some mild damage would be done by us. There'd nearly be war then between the county board and the players before we got on the train.

A bit more cop on was required.

Of course, avoidance isn't always the issue, and some people just don't drink. They're either teetotallers or maybe alcohol is not a good choice for them. But if others want to have a few drinks, then leave them to it. Of course, that's always assuming that everyone understands the limitations of the 'No Drinking Ban' policy. But I don't think players with ambitions of winning an All-Ireland title will make the mistake of crossing that line, and I hope managers are learning to grant players the comfort of just enjoying a few drinks while also keeping their focus on point.

Each player can judge what proportion of alcohol is suitable for them. What works for me might not work for other players. If a person feels violently sick after only a few drinks, then maybe they need to rethink how much they consume. But if you're someone who doesn't get affected by a few drinks, even mentally, then that's a green light for me.

Some people overthink the whole thing and if they play well in a match the morning after having a few drinks, they think their performance was fuelled by the alcohol. That probably isn't the case.

Those few bottles or cans or pints that you had should only be viewed as a relaxant and nothing more. And then others start beating themselves up over enjoying a few drinks if they played badly, as if their bad game couldn't possibly be the consequence of anything else. That's not the right mentality either.

You shouldn't be feeling uptight about this and trying to make connections with drink and performance that really don't exist. They're not related. Having a glass of wine with your dinner is perfectly healthy, whether you're a couch potato or a top county player.

I CAN'T REMEMBER exactly how my All-Ireland eve tradition with Aoife started. Aoife lives in Dublin and would always have a sip on the night after a game. Partly, a drink helped her sleep, but also, it helped her cope with the isolation of living in Dublin and away from all of her teammates in Cork.

I think I'll have a glass of wine.

It was probably as simple as that, and I joined in. It's something we probably both do naturally before a game and this is just a continuation of it. Why should we break our routine just because it's a final? If anything, maintaining your normal pre-match habits are all the more necessary before a game that's as significant as an All-Ireland final.

Sometimes, when you're in the hotel room, there's a lot of hours to sit through before throw-in. You hear of some players who get very little sleep the night before a final. They're up watching TV and are wound up so tightly when they should be getting rest. They're tossing and turning in the bed and can't settle.

That's just energy wasted.

Everyone in our position is excited but nervous, which is understandable, but it's important not to let the anxious energy take over. You must do what you can to relax. It's nice to sit back and have one or two glasses delivered to the room and just completely unwind. You can talk about non-camogie things or camogie-related things either... whatever helps you lean back and kill off some of the anticipation.

I don't want our tradition to be misconstrued. It's not a case of us necking wine, not bothered about the game and 'Party over in our room, lads, come on over'. We're not feeling cocky about the final either.

It's just something we do discreetly and with total respect to the squad.

THE RELATIONSHIP BETWEEN Aoife and myself would be similarly abrasive to the one I share with Paudie. One of us might say something on the pitch that might put the other one out, and it can get confrontational very quickly.

We could drop the hurley at training and have a cut at each other. Even if she's in the right, I would never surrender if Aoife starts barking at me. She never gives me a quarter either. That extends into the club scene as well.

If I'm in my Barr's uniform and Cloughduv are on the opposite side of the pitch, Aoife then becomes my enemy. An opportunity to drill the ball past her is a great chance for a kill.

Aoife and I have hurled with each other from our underage days, and our first encounter on the pitch dates back to the under-12 grade when the Barr's were playing against Cloughduv. I was a substitute that day, coming on at half a foot tall to play in the half-forward line. Aoife was playing in the half-backs. But she always had issues with controlling her breathing, so outfield positions never really suited her.

It wasn't until after she finished playing camogie with Cork that she was diagnosed with asthma. She played on anyway, and left her imprint on Cork camogie before retiring in 2020, with nine All-Ireland medals tucked away.

Her brothers, who regularly used Aoife as a target while pucking about at home when they were young, will probably take the credit for moulding her into a star goalkeeper.

You have to be a bit cracked to play in goals, and Aoife has just the right amount of insanity for the position. She's short, but she has a natural flare for the role. She has the leap of a mountain cat and has great versatility with her hands. She commands her line with total assurance and is always alert to any danger.

Neither is she afraid of getting hurt, so if an opposing player comes charging at her goals, they don't have a good chance in that fight. Aoife never falls short. If she was a bit taller and, perhaps a man, she'd be considered the best goalkeeper that ever played.

At Cork training, we could be verbally aggressive towards each other, and we wouldn't be shy about throwing a few shoulders and a few digs over and back. We're very fortunate that we are very alike but very different, and that makes our relationship work. As soon as training or the match is over, we switch off from the rowing and walk off the pitch having the craic.

We never get personal with the bickering, and even if we do cross the line, we pick up the phone, thrash it out, and drive on again. I'm sure some of our teammates think the dynamic is strange, and the opposition probably ask questions of their markers about the war going on between the centre-back and the goalkeeper.

But that code of honesty is an important part of the foundations in the Cork dressing-room. Aoife and I know that we need each other to be successful, and our mutual understanding of that fact allows us to push each other's buttons without consequences. If you can fight each other here at training, then you'll have a greater fight for each other in a match situation.

That's what we want to instil in the younger girls... be honest with each other, always. That might mean saying stuff you don't want to say out of fear that it could offend them. But if you refrain from addressing the problem, you allow it to grow, and that's much more harmful for the group. Confront the issues now before a match exposes them for you at the most inconvenient moment.

Ultimately, it's good for players to see us challenge each other on the pitch, and still protect our friendship off the pitch. And it's not all roaring and snapping between Aoife and me. We work well together on the pitch too and we always have each other's back. She can read my temperature during a game, and knows how to tug on the reins if I need to be saved from myself.

*****

THERE ARE PROTOCOLS for teams to follow whenever a team wins a final. They're not laid out in the rulebook or anything, but there's an unwritten charter there for winners and losers to follow. Players and management from the winners' corner get their time out on the pitch to celebrate with each other and enjoy the moment in the glow of a victory. Everyone ambles over to wherever the cup is being presented and the good times continue.

There's no manual or set of instructions for the losing team. Your part is over once the final whistle blows… and you're cast adrift. But even in the lulls of a game that doesn't go your way, you have to show respect to the winning side.

We've been on both sides of that fence. And when we lose, we always stand there and watch the cup presentation, regardless of the pain that's coursing through the group.

IT'S THE 2017 MUNSTER final, and we're losing to Limerick in Charleville. We would normally have Limerick's number down, but we're in deep trouble today.

Paudie Murray is normally patrolling up and down the sideline for games like this, but today, as Limerick start to smother us, he decides to take a seat in the stands and get a different view of the game. He's like that massive flaming eye in *Lord of the Rings*, surveying the game from his high tower.

And from his new vantage point, he can see that my tackling technique is not earning me any praise from the referee. The whistle is going almost every time I try to win possession. Paudie uses ear pieces and radio technology to keep in constant communication with his management team. That gear is essential in the modern game to allow managers to make quick decisions and implement them during a game that's moving at a rapid pace.

Paudie discusses my dilemma with his team and decides that I need to move up to full-forward, and away from an area where my supposedly imperfect tackling style could get me sent off for persistent fouling. His brother Kevin is out on the sideline, as are our two runners, Martin 'Mazzer' O'Brien and Seán Cremin, who are on opposite sides of the pitch.

They have to decide who is going to be the brave soul that will prod the beast and tell me that I have to move up to the forwards.

'Seán!' Paudie announces, 'You've got to go in and tell Gemma to go up to full-forward.'

'No, Paudie, not me!' he says pleadingly.

As they continue talking it out, the play switches and I end up on the other side of the pitch in Martin O'Brien's territory. 'Mazzer' is a lunatic. A box of frogs kind of mad.

As well as being a runner for us, Mazzer is a coach for Cork too. Today, he has drawn the short straw to come in and pass on Paudie's instruction to switch. He might be a bit off the reservation, but even Mazzer's not quite cracked enough to be eager about telling me something that might make me pass blood.

'Gemma…' he begins tentatively, 'You're to go up full-forward!'

'Are you having a laugh?' I bark back when I hear about the switch.

Paudie is putting me through a merry-go-round of positional switches again today. He's pulled some wild calls in the past. After the 2015 All-Ireland final, he floored me with the news that I had been nominated to be the sub-goalkeeper for the game. If anything happened to Aoife Murray, I would be stepping in between the sticks for the rest of that final against Kilkenny.

Thankfully, she survived, and that psychotic Plan B idea was never implemented. I don't even know if Paudie was totally serious about that, or if he was just playing mind tricks with me. He has this idea in his head where he sees me as someone who should be on the pitch regardless of my physical condition. Even if both my legs are gone, my presence is enough based on Paudie's mad logic.

He's throwing another one of these grenades today in 2017 against Limerick.

He started me in midfield, and now I'm going up to the forwards. I end going back into the backline which I think sums up the entire day.

We started off really well and whatever happened during the game, Limerick took over and got into their stride. They hit their purple patch and stretched it out for a long time. We fell apart and just couldn't get our shit together. Limerick beat us and we have no choice but to stand and watch someone else lift the trophy.

This is an unexpected defeat for us. Without meaning to sound arrogant, it's almost assumed that Cork will win the Munster title every year. In the Munster Championship, we consider Tipperary to be our closest rivals and we always manage to have enough for them whenever we play them. We would include Limerick in that category of teams we believe we can beat.

It's a scorcher today and Limerick have cooked us.

We expected a win but didn't deliver. They did and it's an historic day for them as they win the Munster Senior Championship for the first time. They scored a goal in the first minute and Niamh Mulcahy finished with 0-11 to edge us out by two points in the end. It's a bit frightening to lose this way, particularly when we can't even point to our performance and say that we're satisfied with how we hurled today.

If we had played reasonably well and Limerick had beaten us, you could at least say, 'Okay, fair enough!' But we don't even have that to fall back on this time.

We were utterly flat and we unravelled at the seams.

THERE'S A SOUR atmosphere in the air, a heavy tension between the players and management. It's full-on in the dressing-room afterwards.

A lot of us are letting it out today... management and players included. We needed to have a fight and get it all out to sort it out. There needs to be some aggravation and someone needs to be ticked off to tease those emotions out of us.

There's no point holding it in when your opinion is needed most, and reserving it for a bitching session in the pub later on. The home truths are spilling out and that's what we need if we want to draw a line under today and improve from here.

There's a slight moment of miscommunication between myself and Kevin Murray where we snap at each other. I want to address the group briefly on the pitch after the game. I call the players over to one side to discuss things before the presentation finishes and people start walking off the pitch.

Kevin misreads what we're doing, and out of concern that people might think we're disrespecting Limerick's moment, he intervenes. He bites at us... and I bite back, pleading with him to relax.

But it's just a brief misunderstanding and we figure it out once we've all cooled down.

But that's more of a footnote on an already dismal day. My big issue is with Paudie's reliance on moving me through different positions. That needs to stop. I can understand the need to make switches but sending me to three different positions in one game? If we're trying to get things done and have a settled unit, three moves in one game almost screams a sense of panic to me. It doesn't make sense and I address that with Paudie in one of our many, many, honest discussions.

These things happen and it's at times like this that the group must sit down, take a breath... accept that changes are needed and start the work to make that happen. Today is one of those little kick-up-the-ass scenarios that can make us a better team down the line.

PART FOUR

WAR DOGS

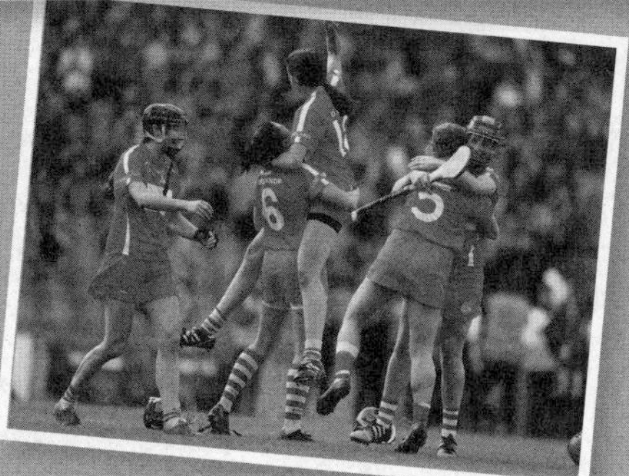

Winning back-to-back All-Ireland titles by a single point over Kilkenny in 2017 and '18 made for a roller-coaster two seasons for Cork. Gemma lifts the O'Duffy Cup in 2017 (top) with teammates, while (middle) Cork present themselves before the 2018 final and (right) Gemma lifts Orla Cotter after winning in 2018.

Despite an invitation from Éamonn Ryan to also build a career on the Cork senior football team, Gemma made the decision to remain focused on her first love, and didn't seek to rival two of the giants of Cork GAA who enjoyed magnificent dual careers, Rena Buckley (top) and Briege Corkery.

CHAPTER 11

We knew if she got through the warm-up, that she would start. But we didn't even know if she could get through the warm-up. The way she carried herself in that game and in the whole month leading up to that game, is the best depiction of the player she was and her will to win. I didn't pay her a lot of attention in that game. You're constantly looking at your players in goals and, by right, I should have been overly conscious of Gemma with her injury. But within two minutes, I didn't have to worry about her. Gemma was just doing Gemma.

– Aoife Murray, Cork camogie goalkeeper, 2017

IT'S ALL-IRELAND FINAL day in 2017 and we've just arrived at Croke Park.

Kilkenny's team bus pulls up around the same time as ours, so we're all heading into the dressing-rooms together. A decision was made last night to start me at 6, but that's information that only the management, myself and my roommate Aoife know for sure.

Everyone else still believes that the knee injury has bested me.

I have a lot on my mind as I go to collect my gear. I'm thinking about the strength of my knee and the strength of my knee strapping, and how I might end up exposing our defence if this whole plan falls to pieces. There's barely enough room in my head for all these thoughts, and now... I see Paudie coming over to tip me over the edge.

'Give me your hurleys and your bag!' he tells me, without explaining himself any further.

'Trust me.'

He just yanks the sticks away from me and scurries off to the dressing-room.

Aoife is beside both of us, laughing uncontrollably at this s**tshow of a sideshow. *Is he actually going out of his way to make me nervous?* So, now I have to walk into the dressing-room with no gear in my hands, a head full of worry... and thinking about how best to murder Paudie after dragging me into his psychological warzone.

It's no use though. I have no choice but to play along with his tricks. Aoife, doing her best to stifle the laughter, offers some advice. 'Gemma, close your eyes, girl, and keep going forward. He's on a mission and you're not going to derail him.'

Paudie continues with the play-acting during his pre-match interview with RTÉ. He swears on the bible that I'm not starting, but that I might get a run if we're three goals up. Guantanamo Bay couldn't torture the truth out of him when he gets going, but if you really study his face during that interview, you can see the hint of a smirk. Just the slightest crease in his skin to give the game away.

I'm looking at him so long that I can read the 'tells' in his expressions. He can't hide much from me. Paudie wants to keep Kilkenny guessing about my situation. As long as they're looking at me, unsure about what's coming down the tunnel before throw-in, it keeps the power in our hands.

If they don't know the truth, then they must have a plan for the possibility of me starting or coming on at some point as a substitute. Or maybe the answer is behind door number three and I'm not fit to play at all, meaning that we've wasted their time.

Uncertainty keeps them distracted from the main thing, which is the game.

One person certainly isn't buying what he's selling though. When Kilkenny manager Ann Downey gets in front of the RTÉ camera before the game, she says that Kilkenny have prepared for me to start, and that it's only in the event of me losing a leg that I won't be playing today.

We can't deceive them and I'm not surprised.

It would be the same if the roles were reversed. I'm a long time playing against

Kilkenny. We have an intimate knowledge of each other and if one of their players had a similar opportunity, they would do the same thing to try and smoke us out. But that doesn't stop Paudie trying to beat them at poker.

*****

THE FIRST 20 MINUTES are a bit of a struggle.

I've tapered back my training for the last three weeks to work on my rehab, and I just feel a bit puffed out. Croke Park on All-Ireland final day is not an arena for baby steps or tiny movements. It's a place where only giant leaps and big strides will do.

To make things even tougher, Paudie decides to put me out at wing-back, a position I haven't played in since my twenties. It's another one of his many tactical calls that I would question. And today of all days, he wants me to revisit my youth.

The orders are to mark Denise Gaule and just do a job to keep her quiet. That's fine, but I'm nervous about this. You're dealing with a player who's a very good hurler and is very switched on. And I'm feeling a bit off the pace. They can unpick the lock with me and run me off the field if they come at me with speed. But Kilkenny's action plan surprises me. Instead of attacking at me, and our defence, they play directly into our hands. They don't push forward to test us out and I'm feeling good as I sweep up all the ball that lands into us.

The strapping is holding everything in place on my knee too.

We brought in Liam O'Reilly last week to wrap me up and let me road test the material to see how much mobility my knee can get from it. I wasn't sure about my condition before throw-in, but I'm relieved to see that everything is still where it should be in the latter stages of the first-half. The other good news is that we're controlling this final and leading by 0-5 to 0-1 after 16 minutes.

We're still three points clear at half-time, but there's some frustration mixed in there for me about that. It's not enough to be just leading against a team of Kilkenny's strength, because that won't kill them off. We should be doing more to press our advantage and leave this Kilkenny team with no way back.

IT'S GREAT TO win All-Ireland finals by one point, but it's also great to be clinical and put your opposition in the ground. It's just disappointing that we were looking good and we didn't push on. We didn't have that killer edge to completely dispatch them.

That would be the ultimate sign off. A statement victory.

It's something we've tried to rectify over the years, but we failed to achieve it. We meet each other again in the 2018 final, where Aoife Murray took a penalty which she would normally drive into the back of the net, but ended up drilling over the bar. I suppose that's the beauty of playing a team that's very similar and equally as talented in every department. There's nothing between us.

Every match-up is a battle to the wire.

Consider a player like Cork forward Amy O'Connor. She's an extremely fast player but when she plays against Kilkenny, she's being marked by someone like Davina Tobin or Grace Walsh. Both of those defenders can probably match her stride for stride over 30 or 40 metres. Amy might be first to the ball, but there's someone behind her breathing down her neck as she goes. She won't get any room to strike the ball.

That means there's a turnover straightaway.

You might have an extra second to consider your next move against other teams in the quarter-final or semi-final, but Kilkenny won't cough up a millimetre of space. The management styles between the two teams are similar too, and probably lean towards defensive tactics in the final phase of games, so it gives very little room to push on. It just bothers me that we allowed Kilkenny back into the game in both of those finals, and created a fight for ourselves that we could have avoided by just driving on.

So, here we both are, coming into the last few strides of the 2017 All-Ireland final and Kilkenny have overtaken the lead and are in front by one point. This is one of the finals that attracts controversial views.

It's low-scoring and highly attritional. The intensity is nauseating.

Everything is a hook, a ruck or a block. It's not a day for fancy flicks or champagne hurling. The purists won't like it. There's 54 minutes on the clock now, as Kilkenny's Miriam Walsh gets the first point in over 10 minutes. That makes it nine points to eight in favour of the defending All-Ireland champions.

Six minutes of normal time remaining.

I'm still on the pitch, with all my strapping still keeping my knee in good shape.

I'm in the ready position. Full-scale ready position. It's key to create movement all the time, even if you don't get the ball. In some patches of the game, you might be in a great position and somebody mightn't see you, but you keep in touch with the play anyway to offer yourself as an option.

Now we're at 59 minutes... and still trailing by one point.

Another ruck forms around the middle of the field and the ball spills out to a Cork hurley. Two passes later and it's in my paw.

Kilkenny players are rushing towards me as I sling my shot over the bar to level the game. Five minutes of added time are announced. My heart is close to exploding out of my chest. *Why the feck do I even play this game?*

This is not good for my health. The stress is ruining me.

JULIA WHITE IS the hero for us today.

She's in a swamp of Kilkenny jerseys when she scores the winner, and I can't understand how she even manages to get the shot off. But it doesn't matter... we're All-Ireland champions again. I haven't a vitamin of energy left.

Weak at the knees and weak in the head... I'm just done for the night. Forget about having a few drinks to celebrate because it would only take one or two drinks to get me drunk the way I'm feeling now. Beating your nemesis in Croke Park when it matters most sends me higher than any drug ever could.

The physical fatigue is worth it.

This is a sweet victory. After everything we went through in 2016... me getting sent off in the All-Ireland final, the manner of that defeat, and just the general misery of that year. Now we're back.

Very little separates us from Kilkenny, and we only get over by a hair today. There's some luck on our side too. Before Julia got that point, Denise Gaule missed a free at the other end. We just have the slimmest edge today.

It's a one-point escape for us, but it still annoys me that we didn't crush them when we had one foot on their neck.

*****

TWELVE MONTHS LATER and we're both back here again... Cork vs Kilkenny in the All-Ireland final for the fifth year in-a-row.

The final is almost a carbon copy of the 2017 game. Scores are at a premium once again and it's another tight contest all the way to the finish. The critics come out with the pitchforks again, attacking the officiating and the defensive playing styles of both teams. It's the main topic that the press want to talk about when Orla Cotter and I are pulled aside for post-match interviews.

One thing that thankfully doesn't make a repeat appearance in 2018, is the strapping on my knee.

DESPITE THE EXHAUSTION after the 2017 All-Ireland final, I did go out and was able to forget about the knee for a while. It was a bit weak and I developed a flare-up of bursitis, which is an inflammation at the back of the knee. Playing the All-Ireland final is probably what caused it.

It wasn't in great condition, but I played in a club game the following week. After pushing through with Cork, I felt I owed it to the Barrs' to strap up the knee and go again. They threw me up front for the game against Ballincollig and I ended up coming off some time in the second-half.

I just couldn't really turn properly on it and the knee was swelling up.

That was my last game of the year and I could fully commit to recovering my knee after that. I took some of the league campaign off to help with that and played my first game of the 2018 season in the league final against Kilkenny. I've always played a full league with Cork, but I needed to let my body recover. Paudie insisted on playing me in the final even though I had just returned to training, and I felt way off the pace in the early stages. I got up to the pitch of it as the game rolled on, but Kilkenny were in great form and those little percentages between us favoured them that day.

I'm not too worried though.

We only lost by one point and the performance was there for us to build on.

MY PREPARATION FOR last year's final was so preoccupied with rehabbing my knee, but this time I can really settle into the excitement of the All-Ireland final build-up. The week before setting off for Croker is such an enjoyable time. It's such a good buzz because training is much more relaxed than the mid-season sessions.

The work is done, and we're just focused on sharpening up on everything... getting attitudes right... getting the body right and getting into the right mode for the final. Everyone has a real pep in their step as adrenaline starts to build within the group. and training is no more than 45 or 50 minutes long.

These types of sessions are really lovely.

About two to three weeks before the All-Ireland final, we typically head to West Cork for some team bonding time. While we're there, we just go training, go to the beach, get coffee and food and play a couple of games. We stay overnight somewhere too. We've been to East Cork for one of those trips as well.

And then we come back to Cork for an open training session and a media night. By now, in September 2018, the knee pain is only a niggle. There's no need for ice machines, MRIs or ringing up Dr Con Murphy looking for a miracle recovery plan. I'm at full power for another round in the ring with Kilkenny in an All-Ireland final.

ORLA COTTER SETTLES it with a last-minute free out near the sideline on the Hogan Stand. We're fortunate to have a player of her talent. Orla is a player I admire greatly, and there's massive respect between us. She sets a high standard with the commitment she gives to Cork and takes great care of the responsibility she has as our primary free-taker.

She always comes to training early to get the practice in, knocking over the dead balls for about half an hour before the session begins. She puts in a lot of unseen hours on her free-taking too. She doesn't panic and is very relaxed when going in to hit the free. She's often had bad days with her frees but so has Cork hurler Patrick Horgan, who's probably the best free-taker in the game.

She's just a calm person and she's quite relaxed generally. Even when she gets frustrated with things in camogie, she never gets too hectic about it. If I'm upset with something, I get hyper about it, but Orla is fairly calm. She's a lady and very chilled out.

You have to be calm if you want to be a free-taker and she exudes cool in stressful situations. She has such a professional attitude and her work ethic is exemplary. A lovely person too.

But our relationship would be different to the one I share with Aoife Murray. We wouldn't be shouting at each other the way Aoife and I would interact on the pitch. Myself and Orla would never speak to each other like that. Now, there might be instances in a game where you get fiery with one another.

'Jesus Christ, Orla… pass the ball. I was free there and you ran into trouble!'

But that's as aggressive as it would get between us.

And that's how it works in teams. Different kinds of relationships emerge for different reasons. You just learn over time what works best for your dynamic. You read their body language and figure out the kind of relationship that will enable you to get the best out of each other. Push each other to be better rather than push each other away.

Every individual is different and you just develop a bond and a style of play that suits you both. And it's important to be respectful to the sensitivities of others too.

That's not to suggest that you should tolerate laziness or bad character in a teammate, but you also can't expect people to only ever act in a way that suits you. You must appreciate that everyone is built differently, and we all have different triggers that stimulate us. So, while Aoife Murray and I would be roaring at each other, I might not go down that road with others because it's not the best way for us to engage with each other.

That's an important learning for management too. Some players respond well to the drill sergeant approach but that doesn't work for everyone. Others need positive reinforcement and the reassurance that they're going well.

*****

IT'S ANOTHER ONE-POINT win for Cork over our rivals Kilkenny.

All-Ireland champions once more.

The celebrations begin on the pitch but they come at a small cost to Paudie as one of the cameramen accidentally jumps into him, equipment first. He's left with a nice thick gash over his left eye, but he smiles and salutes for the pictures anyway.

It's not quite unanimous as to whether the last-minute free should have been awarded or not but, really, we don't care. Yes, it's debatable but then again, the whole game is debatable. Kilkenny were awarded as many frees as us to close out the game and they didn't convert them. But that's not the only moment of the match that seems to be stealing the limelight from our success.

The performance of referee Eamon Cassidy is a major discussion point. The game was a free-fest with Orla Cotter and Denise Gaule playing tennis over and back from dead balls. No flow was allowed in the play, and the lack of consistency in the refereeing is a major gripe for both teams. We don't want this to be the basis of the post-match conversation, but it's all anyone wants to talk about.

Orla Cotter and I are buzzing as the media come to talk to us. But as soon as the recorder is switched on, it's a string of questions about the stop-start nature of the game. You don't mind maybe one person asking about that, but the inquisition is relentless. It's unfair to be asked about it repeatedly.

At the end of the day, it's not our fault and it's not Kilkenny's fault that it was a stunted spectacle. That's a process in itself that has to be looked at and it has been looked at year after year… and they still didn't get it right in 2018. The media are questioning us to add to the debate, but we're only players.

You're quizzing the wrong people about the rulebook.

The child outside playing always imagines themselves scoring the last-minute goal or point to win the game. We're out here living that dream. That in itself is so exhilarating. It's like you're so close to losing and yet, you just about scrape it by the skin of your actual fingernails.

The millimetres that go your way.

That's unbelievable, because there's a fine line between winning and losing, and a puck of a ball could put you on the other side of the result. The way that you step or move your body could have resulted in a decisive free for the opposition. That's the sweetener. Of course it would be nice to be like the Limerick hurlers of today or the Kilkenny from years back and be unstoppable.

But sometimes, winning by a hair, is just the ticket.

*****

THE CORK INTERMEDIATE team also win their All-Ireland final on the same day. Their game against Down preceded our match, and it's their first time to win the competition since 2006. They have even more to celebrate after losing the last three finals in-a-row. It's a special day for all of us.

Two Cork teams coming back home with the spoils of All-Ireland battles. The senior and intermediate squads are part of the same unit. It's the same transport, the same county board set-up, the same managers practically. There's a cross-over of players between the two squads too.

You have to try and forget about the intermediates a bit when you're playing in the senior All-Ireland final, because that's your focus. You're also conscious that if they lose beforehand and you're getting ready to run out onto Croke Park... and Cork have lost, that feeds into your thinking prior to the game. It's the same if they win.

You try to ignore it, but you're only human.

There have been occasions when they've lost and we've won, and that creates an awkward atmosphere in the aftermath. A group of players celebrating beside another group that's grieving. It's unfair to look at a team that has given an equal amount of effort to the jersey and they're on the losing end, while you're trying to have a good time.

That's just the reality of sport. But then if you both win, it's brilliant; it makes for a great weekend. And that's what we have today. It's back-to-back enjoyment.

Paudie is the manager of both teams. That dynamic of having the same manager for both teams is common in camogie but it's a funny one for me. I don't really know how to feel about it. You have a group of talented players who are better than junior but they're not quite at the senior standard yet.

We all train together at the start of the year, and then, coming into the league, the players are divided into the senior and intermediate squads. Some of the intermediates are on the fringes of the senior squad and the rest of the intermediates train together. I don't think it's an ideal set-up. I feel that if you're the senior manager, then that should be your priority. Paudie's life is quite hectic. He is involved in a whole pile of everything. I reckon he spends very little time at home, because he's involved in so much with so many teams. I envy the energy he has... I wouldn't be able for that.

But the arrangement is not practical from a players' point of view. There were some girls who played in the intermediate final, who were then required to line out as a sub on the senior team straight after. I suppose it comes down to the difference between men and women in sport, and where we're at with the development of camogie.

CHAPTER 12

I know Éamonn Ryan was looking for her and I don't say this lightly, but if Gemma put the time into football that she was in a position to do with camogie, she would have been on the Cork senior football team. Gemma was at the peak of her camogie but the way we looked at it, we needed Gemma more than she needed us. She didn't need to play football.

– Mossie Barrett, Donoughmore ladies football manager 1995-2013

IT'S 2009 AND I get an unexpected phone call from one of Cork's all-time sporting greats. It's Cork ladies manager Éamonn Ryan and he wants to invite me into the Cork senior panel.

The Cork ladies are the standard bearers of success in all codes of the GAA. Since Éamonn's appointment in 2004, they have transformed the landscape of ladies football and have become a dominant force in the sport.

They won their first-ever senior All-Ireland title with Éamonn in 2005, and they're aiming to complete a five in-a-row this year. I'm in my twenties, and coming in as a total stranger to the sport. For girls growing up in the city, there aren't many opportunities to play football. It's more of a countryside thing.

I started kicking ball out of a curiosity to try something new, and now I could be on the cusp of something big. I know that this Cork team are going to continue their successful run and there's a possible opportunity there for me to be part of it. The prospect of experiencing All-Ireland success in Football is definitely a tempting one.

I don't know the size or scale of the role that Éamonn has in mind for me, but he wants me to come in and see if it's a fit.

I'VE BEEN PLAYING for the Donoughmore club since 2006. Based near Inniscarra, about 30 minutes outside Cork city, it's home to a couple of my Cork camogie teammates, including Rena Buckley and Mary O'Connor. They're both dual players for Cork too. I considered a few different clubs before settling in here.

I looked at Briege Corkery's club, St Val's, among others, but Donoughmore gets my preference at the end of my search. Their manager Mossie Barrett has been given a tip-off about my interest in playing football from Mary O'Connor, and he rings me up to sound me out. I agree to call up and start training, but I also make it clear from the beginning that camogie is my first priority.

Negotiate the terms before we proceed any further. It's important to ensure that they understand my loyalty to camogie. I'm not here to be the most committed club football player, and if I can't attend something with Donoughmore due to my camogie obligations, then that's just how it has to be. I will attend Donoughmore training when I can.

That's all I can offer because I'm not willing to compromise even a fraction of my commitment to camogie.

It is what it is, but they completely understand my position. Mossie's brother Tomás lives in Cork city and he brings me to Donoughmore training which is a huge help. The arrangement works out really well for me from the start. Mossie and Tomás are great guys and their encouragement gives me a lot of confidence. Playing for Donoughmore is a great opportunity for me to develop as an athlete, and to learn from a collection of proven winners.

This is a club that has done it all. By the end of 2009, they've already won Munster Championships and two senior All-Ireland titles, along with 12 county titles. Donoughmore is also home to some of the best footballers in Cork. I'm picked at midfield which means I get the chance to play alongside the great Juliet Murphy. Juliet is real all-timer for Cork. She played a huge part in helping the Cork ladies team to achieve that breakthrough All-Ireland win in 2005, which ultimately sparked the beginning of a new era of dominance in the sport. Prior to that success in 2005, Cork was really struggling as a county team in ladies football. Club rivalries were a huge factor behind that, and it wasn't until they appointed Éamonn Ryan as manager that Cork began to profit from the potential in their footballers.

My first game is a challenge match against a club team from Kerry.

I'm a bit rusty to start but I quickly find my way. Juliet and myself form a great centrefield combination for Donoughmore, and we split the duties between us so that I take care of the ball-winning and then lay it off to Juliet. She has all the football experience, while I'm fit and eager so we blend well together. We're about four years into our partnership, and everything is going well.

That's when Éamonn makes an approach to see if I'm interested in progressing my football journey to the county grade. Éamonn gives me a call every now and then to sound me out, but from early doors, I make it clear that I don't have the grá for football to pursue it at county level. I'm friendly with Valerie Mulcahy and a few of the players on the Cork team, like Caoimhe Creedon and Regina Curtin, so there would be some familiar faces to greet me if I did decide to go all in. But that's not enough to convince me to make the investment. I know what's required at this level and I just can't give that commitment equally to both Cork camogie and the Cork ladies.

There are a few dual players already trying to maintain that tricky balance. They've been doing it their whole life and maybe the familiarity of it makes it easier for them to keep going. But as an adult starter in the sport, I just don't fancy joining them.

Some time passes before I get another call from Éamonn, and this time, I agree to give it a go but I'm not promising anything. I'm keeping this side project quiet from my camogie folk because I don't want to dramatise it. And there's really no need to admit anything to my camogie teams, as I can already see the end in sight. I head to one or two of the training sessions before shutting the dual-sport project down.

The start of the league is coming up in both football and camogie. As I look at the schedule, and see that Cork are playing in both competitions on the same weekend, I make a firm decision that I am not going down this road. I don't have much time off as it is, because every free second I have goes to camogie. I'm not going to rob myself of what little freedom I have left to take on a new sport at that level.

And to be fair to the football team, my heart just isn't in it. So, I'm just going to leave it at that. It's my call and everyone who knows about this little experiment gives me complete freedom to come to that conclusion on my own. No one tries to dig into my head and sway my vote either way.

THE DUAL PLAYER lifestyle is not an easy one, and I'm not blind to the issues that those players are facing. Fixture clashes are the biggest problem, and it seems like no solutions are forthcoming. Players like Rena Buckley, Mary O'Connor and Briege Corkery are affected by that mess, and they're the ones who are paying the price every time there is a fixture mismanagement. They have tough decisions to make, and there's no right answer to the dilemma.

They're damned if they do, and damned if they don't.

The backlash is inevitable, regardless of what they decide to do. But these players shouldn't have to make those calls. There should be some form of a welfare officer in place to represent the rights of these players and protect them from these scenarios. Relieve them of that headache, and almost take the decision out of their hands.

That's the everyday life of a dual player, and it certainly doesn't appeal to me. Playing at county level is such an intense sport, and that's when you just play in one code. I only attempted such a delicate balance at club level and even that was not a straightforward endeavour. A lot of understanding was required to make it a success.

Donoughmore deserves a lot of credit for accepting my situation and agreeing to proceed with the arrangement on my terms. However, I did worry about how the rest of the squad felt about me being here on those terms. Out of concern for my teammates, I even mentioned my repeated absences to Mossie.

'Look, Mossie… I'm not making training!' I said to him. 'I'm not from Donoughmore. I'm a bit conscious about arriving and playing games when your club players are training hard… and I'm taking a place from them.'

But he gave me total reassurance about it all, and said nobody had alleged that there was any special treatment being afforded to me. In fairness, they have a similar arrangement with the players who are playing for the Cork ladies team.

They understand the dangers of player burnout, and the instruction to them is that Donoughmore don't want to see them when the county season is underway. Mossie is such a successful manager who has guided the Cork men's junior footballers to four All-Ireland titles.

He often manages a few different teams at the same time in the same season, and he can probably relate to my predicament. It wasn't always easy though. There were times when I had to play games and go out training the following day, but they were short spells of discomfort. Overall, I managed to meet all my commitments for the camogie and football teams on my roster.

I can't say I had an illustrious football career, but I also have the relief of knowing that I wasn't burnt out from playing both sports either.

So, that's the scale of the effort involved in pursuing the dual-player life at club level. Imagine the toll it would take on a player if that output was expanded again? That's the reality for some of my Cork teammates. I can see that some of them are wrecked when they turn up for Cork camogie duty. But I suppose the dual sport life is all they've known.

Mary O'Connor has dedicated herself completely to camogie and football. Rena and Briege just get up and do it, and say nothing more about it. Briege would run around all day and never seems to succumb to fatigue. She just operates off her own instincts. You could give her a list of instructions, but they don't always compute in her head, and she'll just go off and do her own thing.

She's partial to a few mars bars on match days. Orla Cotter likes to nosh on them too, but Briege would also have a feed of jellies to go with the chocolate. It's not unusual to see her, sitting on the team bus, munching on the sweets like a child at a party. She's a gas character in many ways, and maybe that explains why she can keep all those plates spinning in the air. She probably doesn't even know she's tired in a game. You could write a book on Briege.

Briege and Rena are always considered as a pair, on account of their fantastic collection of medals across football and camogie. Their attitude and approach as sports people are quite similar but they're very different people on a personal level. Briege has a wildness to her while Rena is quiet.

On occasions when the fixtures collide, the girls would play a game for one of the Cork teams and then travel across the country to play in the other code. There's normally people at one venue, ready to transport them to the other match.

That's such a hectic life to lead, and it sounds like madness to me.

Éamonn's pursuit of me comes up in the brilliant book *Relentless* which documents the legacy of the amazing Cork ladies team, and is written by a great Cork woman Mary White. In it, Éamonn admits that I'm the 'first and only player that he's gone to this length to reel in'.

Obviously, it's cool to have someone like Éamonn making such remarks about you as a player. I suppose he saw me as that type of athlete that he could maybe gain something from for his team. I'm fit, aggressive, and tough, and maybe those are aspects that he wanted to introduce to the Cork ladies dressing-room. He did try to open that door for me, but I just had to be honest with him.

There just aren't enough hours in my life to go around. It's an opportunity that I have to decline, but I also understand what I'm saying no to. The Cork ladies are one of the most successful teams in the history of Irish sport, and they have enjoyed some amazing victories. I'm turning away from the chance of winning a ladies All-Ireland medal with my county. All the possibilities involved aren't far from my mind. Everyone has that road that they didn't take, and this is my one. But there's no other way out of this conundrum. Camogie is going to win that arm wrestle every time.

THE POTENTIAL FOR injuries is a concern for me too.

I've been so lucky in terms of injuries up to now. I tore ligaments in my ankle fairly badly around 2007 or '08 and it took a while to get my body right after that. A few broken fingers and thumbs but nothing that kept me out for the season.

It's not a long list of medical complaints but I have to look at that as a blessing. I have plenty of badges of war from camogie. I don't want to find out what other horrors I could add to that list by bringing county football into the mix.

I don't want to get burned out from all the over-training either.

*****

IT'S 2012 AND I'VE kicked my last ball with Donoughmore. I've enjoyed this experience overall but football just isn't for me on a long-term basis. I've done what I needed to do to get the curiosity out of my system. It was just something I wanted to do for a few years, and have some fun in a new sport.

I don't think I fell in love with the game but I did come away with two county titles and two Munster medals in 2009 and '11 with Donoughmore. We reached the All-Ireland final in 2009 but, unfortunately, didn't add to the All-Irelands' tally. I missed the latter stages of Donoughmore's season due to my overseas deployment in Chad.

After emerging as Cork champions that year, we came up against the great Cora Staunton and the Carnacon club from Mayo in the All-Ireland semi-final. We got the better of them before losing out to Monaghan's Donaghmoyne in the final. It was a great time to be playing with Donoughmore, who were engaged in a tough rivalry with Inch Rovers during those years. The 2011 final was our fourth consecutive meeting in the county final. They were the reigning All-Ireland champions when we defeated them in that decider.

We pressed on to the Munster final where we picked up an eighth senior provincial crown for the club after beating Kerry's Sliabh Luachra, and then lost the All-Ireland semi-final against Dublin outfit Na Fianna. I used to joke with Mossie about how they stopped winning All-Irelands after I arrived, but even without the ultimate prize, this has still been an amazing experience.

I'm sure Paudie Murray admired the ladies team for what they achieved and how, similar to us, they rescued themselves from dire situations. In the last 10 minutes of the 2014 All-Ireland final, Cork famously fought back from 10 points down against Dublin to win. I'm always amazed at the depths of their resolve. But while there's obvious respect there, I don't think Paudie draws too much influence from them in terms of tactics or his managerial approach. Paudie is very much his own man.

Both he and Éamonn are very different managers and they have contrasting personalities in how they marshal their squads. Almost every player who has ever served under Éamonn would say that he has a fatherly approach to the job and endears himself to the group. Paudie wouldn't operate that way and always maintains a distance with everyone in the squad. He openly admits to having a coldness about him when dealing with players.

And in Paudie's mind, detachment yields objectivity when tough decisions need to be made. Every manager has their own coaching style and whatever dynamic produces the best results is the right one for the group.

Some would lean towards Éamonn's way of doing business, and others would agree with Paudie's sterile methods. I've spent a good chunk of my sporting career serving one of them, and if circumstances were different, I could have played for the other too.

There are always the paths you didn't pick, but you'll never miss the turn on the road that's meant for you.

CHAPTER 13

MATHS IS A bit of a block for me in school. They put me into the honours class when I came in as a first year student, but from as far back as primary school, I've always struggled with the subject. I'm eventually moved down to pass level but even then, I still need grinds to help me make sense of the sums, and pass the exams.

I can manage all the other subjects, and I actually quite enjoy history. The study of World War I, World War II and the whole Nazi period really interests me. I find the whole concept of dictatorships fascinating. How can one person with typically evil intentions come to wield such influence over an entire nation of people? It's an incredible phenomenon.

But apart from those specific areas of education, I'm just not built for academics.

Unlike some of my Cork teammates, I can't see myself going down that road professionally. Successful athletes tend to be high achievers in school. The two strengths go hand in hand. A lot of my teammates, who get high marks, are planning to go onto the big universities like UCC. I don't really fit into that category. It's not that I lack the aptitude, I just don't really have the interest to be super intellectual.

There's no real divide in my brain between sport and study... I'm just 100 percent invested in sport. I want to be outside, playing all the time. Mam has a relaxed attitude towards that choice, but dad is less inspired by my approach to school work.

He's the one that orders me to go up and put my head in the books.

I don't despise school, though. Not excelling in the books doesn't mean I can't still enjoy my education. It's a good time here at Presentation Girls Secondary School near my home in Ballyphehane. And it's good people too. I can't speak for the country schools but when you attend schools in the city, you end up sharing the corridors with a whole array of people from different backgrounds.

Good backgrounds, bad backgrounds and middle of the road people are all represented in these halls, and I find it easy to mix with all of them. I feel relatable to everybody, from the studious to the non-studious pupils. Our social groups aren't based on our grades. I can hang out with everyone.

I think being a talented athlete really helps me build friendships too. Playing for Cork and winning for Cork does earn you a bit of respect in school. Of course, there's the odd few who say, 'Oh Gemma, you think you're great'. But the slagging is all harmless really… just a bit of a laugh. I'm not a bother to the teachers really, but I do enjoy the chats and the craic. I had a brilliant relationship with the principal of our primary school Mrs Fitzsimons. She was also a close friend of my mam's.

In secondary school, I have a teacher called Ms Treacy who likes to tell me, 'Jesus Gemma, I could kill ya… but I'm so fond of ya!' Our principal Sister Sheila, and vice-principal Mr O'Mahony, are both huge supporters of mine. They recognise all of my achievements in major games, either by announcing it over the intercom or in front of a school assembly. Gestures like that mean a lot when you're young, and those acts of kindness stay with you as you get older. And since I'm not great at keeping my head in the books, sport is one avenue that allows me to give something back to my school.

FOR A LONG time, I didn't know what I wanted to do with my future. I felt like I didn't have any direction because of that. But I think at this point, as I head towards fifth year, I'm starting to realise that I need to pick a path that promises some kind of involvement in sport. I considered joining the guards at one point.

There's lots of moving about in that job, but I'm not entirely sold on it. It's not until I run into someone while they're handing out pamphlets in town, that I start thinking about a future in the Defence Forces.

One of my aunts is married to someone who works in the navy, so I decide to have a chat with him, to find out if there's a future for me in this. His first piece of advice is to steer clear of the navy because I would be out at sea a lot, meaning you can't get much leave to go training. That obviously won't work for me, so he suggests giving the army a go.

I'm still not completely ruling out the guards, but now that I have the Leaving Cert behind me, I'm going to start my application process for the army. I go for my interview before doing a fitness test and a medical check. There's a two-week induction phase after that. That's where people come in with their parents and everyone is put into a briefing room where the platoon sergeant and platoon commander come in and make the introductions.

You get briefed on what's ahead of you. The induction phase is a taster, a brief introduction to military life. You learn things like how to fall into march and the general basics of a soldier's life. You're given an army tracksuit, a pair of runners and you're sent down to the gym where you meet the physical training instructor.

Those two weeks have the biggest drop-out rate because that's when a lot of recruits realise they don't really like it and that the army life isn't really for them. That's always puzzling to me, because those first few weeks are just the starter pack. The real tests are still ahead of you. Recruits who leave early say things like, 'Oh, I didn't know we had to be up at this time'. But if you make it through those two weeks, and you realise you love being in the army, then it's off to recruitment training. There's four months of the initial training and then another two months of a different phase of training. The beginning is tough but enjoyable too. I'm enlisting straight after sitting my Leaving Cert so I have youth on my side, and buckets of energy to withstand the training.

It is very regimental and structured but I like those aspects of the army. I like the way you pack your kit in a nice and tidy fashion. Everything is in its place. You're up in the morning and on programme straightaway. You begin with your physical training in the morning or afternoon, and you also have all your weapons training and map reading during the day. You do all your drills and your ground phase which is basically your tactics out on the ground. There's some theory work involved with our training too.

As part of some of our courses, we have to conduct a presentation on a topic of our choosing, or a military leader. Irish history is packed with examples of people who fought for our independence, and helped to shape the foundations of our great country. We always hear about the work of Michael Collins and James

Connolly and Pádraig Pearse, but there are other leaders to explore. I want to look at the women who were equally significant to the Irish cause, and so I decide to focus my presentation on the life of Countess Markievicz.

I always knew who she was but, I suppose, while doing the research on her background more in-depth, I became more interested in her legacy. Countess Markievicz came from such a prestigious background and left it all behind in the name of the Irish cause. And the public loved her. That's such a noble and selfless act that has echoed through the course of our history.

When she died, the whole of Dublin lined out to honour her memory. She was a protestant but a nationalist and a very wealthy woman. She was one of the original suffragettes in Ireland and I was drawn to all of that. It's nice to look beyond the surface level of history and recognise the women who made equally huge contributions to the national effort. There are other leaders who aren't just men. My presentation about Countess Markievicz is my tribute to that.

THE GENDER RATIO in the Defence Forces is very male-heavy, and less than seven percent of the members are women.

Some women don't consider joining the army because they think it's a bit misogynistic or that it's too male focused. I know my life is completely different to somebody else's so what's meant for me might not be for someone else. This is just the path that I have chosen to go down.

There were five girls in my platoon out of a class of 36 when I started, and we all finished together. One of those girls moved abroad with her husband a few years after finishing recruitment training. The number of women in the army has always been small, and it's getting smaller. Some platoons might have only one female in the ranks. Being outnumbered by the male recruits doesn't bother me, but the isolation can be part of the reason why a lot of women leave the army.

When you finish your programme at the end of a day's training, you return to your billet which is your living quarters. That's where you can have a bit of craic and feel normal for a while with the people you're living with. That dynamic works if there's four or five people all there together. But if you're the only woman in a platoon, you have to go back to the accommodation by yourself.

You can't live with the lads because there's a very strict policy about the male and female lines and keeping them separate. There are no restrictions on romantic relationships forming between troops, and some couples even travel overseas on peacekeeping missions. But they still have to obey those accommodation rules while on tours of duty.

Being in a billet by yourself is very lonely after a hard day. You're obviously away from your family too. And for that reason alone, women drop out.

People who don't know anything about the Irish Defence Forces think it's a joke. They don't think it's a legitimate unit of the military because we're not out on the front line in Afghanistan or in some other war-torn place. Some people even join the Defence Forces with that kind of uninformed attitude. They completely underestimate the training, which far exceeds the standard of other nationalities.

However, they end up paying for their ignorance when the training starts. Our training is very robust and it's hard. Of course, you must be physically fit, but you also have to be mentally tough to dog it out. That's what it means to be part of a team.

Women often demonstrate that toughness really well. We might not be the fittest or the strongest, but we have a kind of mental stubbornness embedded in our mindset. That's what helps you survive the training. It all comes down to an individual's mental state and whether you want to be there or not. If you don't want to be there, it's going to be physically and mentally horrible. The reward and enjoyment comes from wanting to be there, despite the physical toll.

And you're part of a team… you're not out there by yourself. You depend on the team and the team depends on you. If you're not pulling your weight, you're letting everyone else down… and being what we call a 'mé féiner.' If you're in a part of a platoon and you f**k up, then that has an effect on everyone's training that day.

So, it's in everyone's best interests to give it your best.

Some soldiers, particularly those who join before or after college, leave once they've had their fill of the overseas tours and the bit of life experience that the army can impart to them. A little burst of maturity to send them on their way into adult life.

The contracts are slightly different now too. I was one of the last groups to join that could get the old 21-year pension. At 38, if I really wanted to leave the army, I could, and I would pocket a pension with that. But those pensions don't exist in the Defence Forces anymore. They're not included in the post-2004 contracts.

Now, it's like any other job, and you have to put the grind in until you're 62 or 63 to get a normal pension. It's not that there's no incentive to stay in the army, but I can understand why people leave if they're not satisfied with the paying conditions.

*****

OVERALL, THIS LIFE works for me.

I'm still employed by the army and I've never lost my place on the Cork team. There are always challenges to face, but the freedom to comfortably balance my life between army duty and camogie is a big plus for me. I'm always accommodated. No blocks are placed in front of me.

Sport and the Defence Forces complement each other, and to my employers, they see me as representing the Defence Forces when I play for Cork.

At the start of each year, I try to fit in as many work-related projects for the army as possible. I'm building up credit in the bank to use when I need time off for camogie later on in the year. By around June, I start to taper off the army circuit slightly as the championship campaign starts ramping up. With all the work I've done, I can feel confident about requesting time off for a match that's coming up. When you work in the army, you get out what you put in.

You have to be proactive about getting the most out of yourself as a soldier. If you want, you can happily go in, sit on your laurels and have no initiative. But if you want to do stuff, you have to make that happen for yourself. I don't want to develop a reputation for being lazy, so I max out my effort for the army when the camogie season is a bit quieter. I work hard here, so I can play hard for Cork.

One of the highlights is when I am selected to go to Paris Island in Carolina as the only female instructor to visit the U.S. Marine Corps. I was there for two weeks as part of a four-man team to review how the marines train and compare their methods with our own.

Army work can be difficult, but more importantly, my job is very flexible and I get plenty of time off when I need it. It's not always easy to manage though. The work-athlete life balance can be tiring when there's a lot of energy output involved in both activities. On one occasion, I played in a county final the evening after finishing a course that was quite physical.

We spent hours in the mountain as part of that course. You can sometimes come off duty feeling exhausted, and have little time to rest before going out to play a game. And that game could be something as significant as a Munster final. Coming home from an overseas tour can present some difficulties too. You've been in a bubble for six months and now you're trying to fit back into your old routine again. That can take some time.

I might be coming home with a good bank of fitness, but that's only relative to what you're doing. I'm coming home feeling gym fit but perhaps not match fit. As a general recruiter, the training sometimes involves carrying weights and that can slow you down and affect match sharpness. It can take a while to readjust when you have those little quick transitions over and back.

And then there are times when I just can't keep my camogie and army schedules apart.

*****

IT'S 2013 AND I have to miss a chunk of the camogie season to go on a peacekeeping mission to Lebanon. This will be my third trip overseas after going to Liberia in 2004 and Chad in '09. The Irish Defence Forces have been travelling to Lebanon on peacekeeping missions since 1978.

In that time, 47 Irish troops have died while on a tour of duty there. That's a significant death toll which we mark every month with a ceremony during our own tours to acknowledge their passing. In 1978, Lebanon was a country torn by conflict and violence. There was a civil war in Beirut, and a conflict was raging between Israel and Palestine. Attacks were taking place along the southern Lebanon border. Israel later invaded Lebanon, resulting in the deaths of innocent people in Lebanon, Israel and Palestine.

The first Irish peacekeepers were deployed to south Lebanon under a UN mandate to supervise the Israeli withdrawal from the country, and ultimately, restore peace over there. That effort to achieve stability in the area is still ongoing. The fighting has lessened over the years, but the threat is still there.

I've already missed out on some opportunities at work and I can't put this off any longer. I'm leaving in May, meaning I'm going to be deployed for a lot of the big championship games. I explain this all to Paudie and tell him that I'm due to travel overseas, and that I need to box this tour off sooner rather than later. I don't particularly want to go but I need to do this to put myself in line for promotion opportunities.

You just can't avoid the tours forever.

These trips technically run on a voluntary basis but there's a running joke in the army that you're 'voluntold'. If you don't put your hand up for these trips, you could end up going as a mandatory selection. That happens when there's not enough positions filled or there's a certain skill-set required on the mission that isn't already present among the soldiers who have volunteered.

The army has been downsized in the last few years and the retention rate has been really low. They're finding it hard to fill those vacancies, so troops who are on post-2004 contracts can be a mandatory selection. I'm voluntold for this trip, but I'm also overdue to go on tour, so I knew this was coming.

There's money to think of too in all this.

Camogie doesn't pay the bills.

I'm in the B Company for this trip, conducting small short-range patrols around the AO (Area of Operations). They will assign us to a specific part of the AO for us to drive through. These patrols can take hours to complete, passing through different villages as we go. This is a different role compared to the work I was doing on my tours to Chad and Liberia when I was tasked with long range patrols. Those expeditions could keep you out on the road for six to eight days.

Again, we passed through different locations before setting up a patrol harbour to foot patrols in that area, create a presence and communicate with the local mayors. During my time in Chad, we had a permanent base where we had to travel to an outside post area to maintain our presence for a week or two weeks. We had a tiny camp, and operated our foot patrols and mobile patrols from there. Sometimes we went by foot, and other times we travelled by chopper.

Similar to Liberia, we lived in a hot climate but it was a dry kind of heat. Desert-like conditions. We also had to endure extreme switches in temperature.

I was on patrol in a place in Chad which was in the middle of the desert. At night, from about 10pm onwards, until 4am or 5am, the temperatures would plummet. To help us through that, we wore jackets called snugpaks which are almost like sleeping bag material. We wrapped ourselves in those and cocooned in the tents with quilts. We originally slept in one-man bivi tents, but a doctor made the call to replace them with six-man tents due to the threat of snakes and scorpions in the area.

In the morning, we put a big pot of porridge on the gas cooker for breakfast. But by six or seven o'clock, the hot sun would emerge to cook us all again. By 9am, the temperatures were soaring to 30 degrees.

Freezing one minute, boiling the next.

*****

I GET HOME in time for the 2013 All-Ireland semi-final against Kilkenny at Semple Stadium in August. I've never been dropped for Cork, and despite my absence, Paudie wants me to play. I'm reluctant to agree.

I don't want my teammates to see me as someone who just saunters back into the team, and I also don't want to take the place of someone who has been delivering for Cork throughout the championship. Paudie assures me that the girls want me back in the side and that this is the best decision for the team.

He doesn't pressure me into it but I am conscious of the fact that I'm army fit rather than match fit. There's an important difference and I just don't know how much of an asset I'll be. I agree to play, coming on in the 55th minute of the game, but my 2013 championship starts and finishes there in Thurles, as Kilkenny beat us by one point to progress to the All-Ireland final.

PART FIVE

MAM

Gemma at three with her mam Geraldine, after getting the red wellies she had 'pestered' for, and (below) mother and daughter all glammed up in 2003 for the Star newspaper awards night in the Guinness Storehouse in Dublin.

The 'good times' as Geraldine (top and middle) relaxes with family and friends and (left) Irish Examiner *awards come the way of Gemma and her 'Right Hand Woman'.*

CHAPTER 14

IT'S THE 2014 ALL-IRELAND final and my legs are like jelly.

They could turn to mush any second now. It's us versus Kilkenny... the first chapter of our Holy War.

We have four more days like this in Croke Park to look forward to over the next four years. This is basically Christmas Day for camogie. The stadium rumbling, cogs rattling off the tunnel like raindrops, skin flying, hurleys clattering... that's adrenaline straight into my mainline.

All the sounds I live to play for.

We haven't held the O'Duffy Cup in five years, and we want it back.

A day like this should thrill me, but my head is somewhere else. It's been wandering for weeks. At training, I'm there... but I'm not all there. I'm plugging through the motions for this weekend.

Basically, non-committal.

I'm just floating really.

Is any of this really all that important? Playing sport and training like dogs in the hope that you might get a bit of tin at the end of the year.

What's the point? What does it matter?

The worst that can happen to us here today is we might lose a match. We might have to wait another year to try to win the All-Ireland. Years we have. Big deal. *Where does a disappointment like that really sit in the big picture?*

Tears will fall for a day or two and then we'll move on. There'll always be another chance. No one dies here.

She doesn't have those years.

Why her? Why did it have to be her?

It's such a small, tiny, non-important thing, this game we play.

Sport is just sport.

*****

I'M AT WORK on a Thursday evening when I receive a call from my mother. She's ringing from the bus.

'I'll be fine,' she says reassuringly. 'I just want to go in. I still have that pain, and I have that letter from the doctor.'

It's not normal for her to take the bus but she's using it today, and is on her way to Mercy University Hospital (MUH) in Cork city. I offer to leave work and bring her in myself, and spare her the misery of an uncomfortable bus journey when she's not feeling well. But I can tell from her voice that she just wants to get there and get this looked at.

A few weeks ago, as she was travelling to a funeral with Aoife and myself, her back was in agony. I could see she was in pain as she climbed into the car. First signs only become first signs in hindsight... they don't stand out at the time.

Thinking it was a muscular issue, mam relied on the chemist for relief, but the pain wouldn't ease up. Sometimes that happens with the symptoms. They're just lurking around in the system before the discomfort kicks in to give you any concern. The alarm bells ring too late. I don't think she was afraid of going to the doctor, although it's rare that she ever needed to see one.

She's been in good health up to now, apart from a bout of pleurisy and pneumonia in the lungs that she told me about from when she was around 19. She was a smoker for years and that was her crutch, but she's off them now. She hasn't smoked since just before I was deployed to Lebanon last year.

Maybe that was too late a time to give them up.

Her GP believes her pain might be related to an issue with the gallbladder. That's what he told her the first day when she called in to get looked at. He was going on holidays that day, but left a referral letter for her to bring to A&E if her symptoms continued to persist.

And now, armed with that letter, she's taking the bus to hospital where she gets admitted later that night. She has to wait a long time before she gets seen by anyone, but now that they have, they want to keep her in overnight.

I'm a bit out of sorts as I hang up the phone, worrying about why mam is going to the hospital so urgently? *Maybe she just wants to get something sorted?* Mam is tough and has a high pain threshold, and she might just need help to shake off the pain, and maybe there's nothing to worry about.

All I can do is guess what she's thinking. Mam's a deep person with deep intuitive thoughts, and she doesn't give herself away.

IT'S FRIDAY AND I'm in work again in the Brigade Training Centre (BTC) in Cork. I'm giving the place a hoover and a clean before clocking off. It's around quarter to four. My boss, who is the commanding officer here, has just come in with his daughter.

Fridays are half-days at the BTC, but the place is quiet and empty, so I'm just giving it a quick sweep before heading off.

My phone rings. It's my dad.

'It's not good at all, Gemma!' he explains.

'They're after finding a tumour in her lungs!'

Tumour is not something I have any experience with. That word has never been uttered in our family. Dad's sister has recently been diagnosed with a brain tumour, but this is the first time my immediate family has been affected by an illness of this scale. It floors me straightaway. I'm down but somehow still standing.

I just can't reconcile the news with the woman I know. Mam has always been healthy, super fit and bursting with life. She walks everywhere, tearing up the roads as she goes. Cork city is about a 25-minute walk from our house, but that's no distance to her. She's never even been in hospital like this before. I've never seen her get winded by anything.

It's impossible to rationalise any of this. I rush to the toilet, inconsolable. I'm conscious that my boss is still outside and I don't want to see anyone right now. I wait for him to leave while I try to process everything. He's a lovely man and I'm sure he would do his best for me if I told him, but I need to take this in by myself before facing anyone else.

I get to the Mercy Hospital and all my family are there. My mam's sisters, my dad, Glenn... they're all here. I'm drifting out of my body as everything is happening around me. Surreal. Floating around.

A priest comes down the corridor, looking for Glenn and myself, wanting to talk to us about the news that our family has just been crushed by. That's not a good sign, and I haven't even seen my mam yet.

But then, what do you even say to someone that you love and care about so much, after they've been given such devastating news? She's heartbroken. Completely. There's a biopsy scheduled for her tonight, to confirm the extent of her tumour.

But there's not much left to determine. The scans that they've done so far have already uncovered a lot of the damage. The next step is to see an oncologist to find out a bit more about her condition.

*****

THE FIRST 20 MINUTES of the 2014 All-Ireland final go by in a haze. I'm lost on the field, trying to find my feet and having no luck. Now it's half-time and Kilkenny are leading by five points.

I can't decide whether that's down to nerves on our part, or Kilkenny's ability to establish a purple patch and keep capitalising throughout the course of the half. Either way, they're on top at the halfway point. They're fired up and we're not getting a spark.

I'm doing my best to focus on the game, but mam's appointment with the oncologist is in a few days. This final is not an occasion for me to exert any major influence on the game. My focus is on doing the simple things right, fulfilling my role, and finishing the job. That's all my mind can handle right now with everything else that is already packed into my head at the moment.

Is this all really happening?

WE HAVE A habit of starting games slowly and it's happening to us again.

We're all so aware of it. It's a real bone of contention in the squad, and everyone realises that as we enter the dressing-room to regroup and re-organise. 'It's not an option to lose against Kilkenny. We haven't even started yet!'

That's the message echoing through the room.

Get that slow start out of our system and switch on the engine. We have our orders and we know what to do. From that moment on, we put the ghosts of the first-half behind us and get going.

Croke Park is such a powerful stadium, and it can make a player feel powerful. It gives us that charge of energy for the second-half. We were anonymous in the first-half, and now, suddenly, we're alive and well in this contest. Croke Park brings out that desire in us. The under-performance in the first-half has left us with no option but to come out in the second and correct those mistakes.

We're roaring to life now, and there's a two-point advantage to our name in the 59th minute. Of course, Kilkenny have no intention of going out with a whimper. There's no surrender with them, as Miriam Walsh delivers the ball into our penalty area from around midfield. Denise Gaule gets underneath it.

She clips the ball in towards the goal where I'm holding guard, and a group of us swarm towards the loose possession like beetles. These kinds of rucks in front of the goal can go any way.

One stray swing from nowhere could send the ball fizzing past Aoife Murray in goal.

The ball pops out to Kilkenny's Aoife Neary as I crash into her, just inches from the goal line. She fumbles the ball but has a second go at it and tries to palm the ball into the net with one last effort.

Thankfully, we manage to scramble it away from danger as our corner-back Joanne O'Callaghan scoops the ball into her chest and breaks clear. She gets a bang on her wrist on her way out. The referee awards us a free.

Aoife Murray screams out encouragement and throws up a few fist pumps to reinforce our authority in this game. Kilkenny come surging forward again a minute later, but again, they come away with no change.

Our defence is just a red wall in front of Hill 16.

They may have rattled us in the first-half, but we're coughing up nothing now.

*****

MY TEAMMATES ARE so supportive. They know how to read the temperature when they're around me, and give me what I need at that moment.

Some players come up and try to talk to me about it, others know when it's time to step back and give me some space. I'm one of the oldest players on the panel, which makes it difficult for some of the younger ones. Sometimes, they don't know what to say.

One or two of the senior players acknowledge the situation with me, and some even tell me about their own experience of cancer coming into their home. I appreciate the effort from everyone, but in those cases, their parents got a cancer diagnosis and came out the other side. I just know, in my heart of hearts, that mam is in a different position. But I can also draw some comfort from their stories. It does help to know that we're not the only family that has been through it. We're not alone. There's probably families all over the world going through the same thing that we are right now. But when you're in it, it's very hard to compare your situation to what other people are going through.

Throughout it all, Paudie Murray is doing his best to keep the show on the road. Maintain some normality for me, and for everyone else. Matthew Twomey has been, and continues to be, very good to me. Sometimes you just need space to have a cry or a vent for five minutes. Just to release some of the emotion and the hurt. Matthew is there to help me with that. He lends the ear whenever you need to have that kind of conversation.

We end up winning the All-Ireland final by six points thanks to a last-minute goal from Angela Walsh. It's so satisfying to win by that margin after our heads were left spinning at half-time.

We've waited five years for this moment… to reach the top of the mountain and put Cork camogie back where it belongs. We're finally at the peak, putting our flag in the ground. I should be buzzing.

And, ordinarily, I would be buzzing on a day like this.

I normally feel so free after winning an All-Ireland final. And an 11-point turnaround is such a testament to the resolve in this team. But it's just not registering with me. There's no sense of elation. No euphoria.

No relief.

We get back into the dressing-room and the good times are in full swing. Rapturous cheers of joy and triumph fill the room. But I'm on mute. I'm just sitting down, not celebrating with anyone.

I'm oblivious to what the girls are doing and they're oblivious to what I'm doing for that split second. Elaine Burke and Úna O'Donoghue, two former Cork teammates of mine, come in to congratulate me and sympathise about my mam's condition. A message of joy and pain, all in the same breath.

It feels so strange to have all these opposing emotions running in tandem in my head. I'm just going through everything, thinking about what this all means.

This all seems so *insignificant.*

But that's when it hits me. It does matter.

All of this matters. It matters to her, and that's why she's here. She might not be here again for another All-Ireland final trip. But she's here *now,* despite everything that she's going through. I have to do it for her, and I *did* it for her.

Because it all starts with her. I run up to my mam in the stands after the final whistle and give her a hug. I always go to her after the final whistle of every game. I hold her lightly in my arms, careful not to squeeze her too tight.

It's a surreal moment for her too, knowing what lies ahead. I still feel so removed from everything.

THE HOMECOMING IS normally my favourite part of the celebrations. It's such a special and intimate time.

You're coming back to Cork, with the trophy over your shoulder, ready to start enjoying the achievement with your own people. You have something to show for the grind you've put in over the season.

It's always been the tradition to stop off at Mallow train station on the way home and get a reception there. We then pull into Kent station and get on an open-topped bus to the Mall, where there's another reception in one of the hotels.

We get on a stage then and there's a good reception there.

We then head to the captain's club and let the craic begin. But this time, as soon as I get home, all I want to do is be with mam and my family.

I just want to get her in to see the oncologist.

*****

IT'S A FEW days after the All-Ireland, and we're in the office of Dr Derek Power, mam's oncologist, to get a clearer understanding of her diagnosis. There's a lot to take in but there's only a few words that I hear.

Stage 4.

Terminal.

Non-operable.

To give it the full title... it's Stage 4 non-small cell lung cancer.

Inoperable.

That word carries the biggest punch. Having no option to operate removes all reason to be hopeful. We would take any chance of being able to fight this. Give us a 50/50 shot, or even 60/40. You can believe in the odds, no matter how much they're stacked against you. A chance is a *chance.*

But to be sitting in front of the oncologist, basically confirming our worst fears, is devastating. They put a treatment plan in place for mam, which includes a course of chemo.

We won't be seeing the oncologist again until January.

We go outside, the three of us, and drive home where my aunts and uncles are waiting for us. It feels like we're starting the grieving period already. We all go back home to Ballyphehane and sit outside together in the garden. It's a lovely September day, and the last whips of the summer sun are coming over us.

But any relief we could get from the weather is playing second best to the pain, and the devastation, and the hurt that we're all feeling for this person that we love. We're all just coming to terms with the fact that this is it.

Glenn couldn't attend the meeting with the oncologist and we have to tell him when he gets home. I watch his face as he tries to take it all in. 'She'll be able to fight this,' he says, doing his best to cling to some hope.

I wouldn't wish any of this on my worst enemy.

Mam loves life, loves her kids, her family and her sisters. There are eight girls and two boys in her family and they're all extremely close. She's a twin with her sister Liz, and the pair of them are like two peas in a pod. She's not done with this world yet and, at the same time, she's being ripped away from it.

'I've so much to live for,' she tells me. 'I'm 54 years of age. I don't want to die!'

I know she'll fight this with every inch of her strength, and she has to believe that there's some hope. She doesn't want to waste a second in getting her treatment started at the end of the month.

Before starting the chemotherapy, mam has a few tests to get through, including a stress test on the heart. There's one intravenous session of chemo at the start, and then everything comes in tablet form after that. She's feeling okay after the first few rounds, and there's 12 weeks of chemo altogether in her treatment plan.

The first few rounds remain okay for her but the side effects soon arrive. She starts feeling nauseous and her hair starts to fall out. My mam had thick, jet black hair. She loved her hair and loved to style it with all sorts of colours and cuts.

It's a short cut now, but when she was younger, she had long voluminous hair that was very like the look of the singer Kate Bush. Deep reds and purples were some of her favourite choices.

And now I'm watching her as she has to feel it all come out strand by strand. The hurt keeps coming. She starts wearing these really cool bandanas, and has a wig too. There's a wig clinic in Cork, which mam speaks really highly of and the staff are great to her.

They fit her with a really cool wig, which looks great on her. She wears it to the All Stars and a few other events, but she hates the material because it irritates her scalp. So she doesn't wear it that often.

The bandanas offer mam an alternative way to still be stylish without her hair. She just loved hair and how it enabled her to craft her own individual style with it. Losing her hair felt like she was losing so much of herself and the artistic side of her life.

When women lose their hair, it takes away some of their individuality and their signature look. They're so used to their hair and whatever way they want to wear it. It's a form of self-expression. The hair you're born with doesn't have to be your look for life. There's great power in restructuring it and dressing it up or dressing it down, whichever way you like.

And without your hair, your appearance is totally different. What you show to the world, and what people normally see of you, has vanished and you're just left with your scalp. I couldn't believe my mam's beautiful hair was slipping away from her.

The bandanas help her to replicate her personality with all the colours and styles. They're edgy too, just like her hairstyle. She could wear any colour she liked and they would suit her, and the shape of her face. The bandanas are giving her back some of what she's lost through her treatment.

For some, their hair might even be a cloak or protection against the outside world and now that wall has collapsed, leaving you feeling exposed. It's not even a case of losing the hair... the sickness and the treatment is taking it away from her. A woman without her hair feels like a certain amount of their femininity has been torn from them.

It's so hard to deal with that, and probably people who suffer from alopecia feel the same way. Wearing a bandana helps mam to restore some of her power.

*****

IT'S A TUESDAY in January 2015, and we're back with the oncologist in the Mercy for an update on mam's condition, and to find out how she's reacting to the treatment.

'Geraldine,' he starts, 'today's a great day. The tumour is after shrinking greatly.'

What? I can't believe what we've just heard.

Is that possible? Are you sure?

This is the best type of disbelief. This is massive for mam.

She was given a time period when she first went into the Mercy. I wasn't told about those details of her prognosis at the time, and honestly, I didn't want to know how much time she had left. But, now, I don't think I need to know. Oncologists speak very abruptly and they don't sugar-coat any of the details when they're speaking to patients about their condition. So, if he's calling this a 'good news day', then we have every reason to be optimistic for mam. His words illuminate her face and completely lift her spirits.

We've just won the lotto with news like this. That hope we've been searching for, scrapping for... that seemed so out of reach, is finally here. To what degree, we don't know yet, but everything seems possible for her again.

Maybe she could live with this for a couple of years? The oncologist says her tumour has shrunk, and maybe it might stay that way?

The other good news is that the oncologist says that we can take a break from the chemo and go away on a holiday, and basically do whatever we like. For the first time in a while, we have permission to enjoy life. My aunts were afraid to come into the city today but as soon as we get out of the hospital, I ring them up to tell them the good news.

There's some happiness and excitement back in our family again as we all head out to Kavanagh's for food. Things feel normal again, even if it's just a small bit of normality. The fear hasn't completely vanished, of course. Mam's tumour is still there and we still don't quite know where we are with her treatment.

No one is underestimating the long road that still lies ahead of us. We get home that night and I'm wrecked and happy all at once. As my head hits the pillow, I feel free to close my eyes and enjoy my first peaceful sleep in a long time.

These few weeks of living normally are amazing and mam feels good. Her hair is even starting to grow back again. It's coming back in the form of curls in a kind of dark colour somewhere between black and grey to replace the jet black strands of her former look. My uncle John is a hairdresser with a salon in town and he's planning to style it. He styles all my aunts' hair as well.

We organise a trip to Kenmare for the whole family. Mam, my aunts, my nan, my cousins and Aoife are all coming along. It's nice for mam to get a break and she seems to be in good form with the way she's talking.

'I'm actually really lucky that this is after working,' she tells us one day in Kenmare while we're all in the hot tub. It's great to hear that positivity in her voice after the horrible few months she's been through.

There's another scan coming up in the summer, and we'll know more then.

*****

THE CONSULTANT TRIES to explain what has caused this.

From reading the scan, he can see that the tumour has sort of mimicked itself to hide from the chemo, and trick the chemo into thinking that it's doing its job. So, while mam was taking a break from the treatment, so was the tumour.

We just couldn't tell.

It started to grow again during that time and just didn't stop.

The news isn't a complete surprise. I sensed that mam was a bit off before we went to Kenmare. She didn't say anything but her form was just different and I figured she might be in pain. She became unwell again during the holiday and that worried her too, thinking of what the symptoms might be telling her about her condition. I was frightened too, and I had an inkling that things weren't as good as we thought they were.

And now there's no doubt.

Now, we know exactly where we are, and our hearts have been shattered all over again. The few weeks of hope have now been wiped out. We've had our worst fears confirmed a few times already, but this is the lowest we've felt after an update about her condition.

IT'S JULY, AND mam and I head out to the Regional Park in Ballincollig for a few pucks. It's what we love to do, and what we've always done.

It's just the same as when we go down to Stiofáin Naofa or to any of our other favourite hurling haunts. We bring my puppy Molly along for the walk too.

It's a beautiful day, and mam is swinging the hurley over and back, smacking the ball as the sun beats down on us. She looks great with her headband on, and she feels good too.

We know where we're at with everything that's happening, but as I look at her, all I can see is someone who's having a fun day out. Free from the pain.

It's great to see her smiling, even if it's just for today.

CHAPTER 15

IT'S 2019 AND our season is over after an All-Ireland semi-final defeat to Galway. For the second time in my career, I'm the captain of a Cork team vying for a three in-a-row that fails on the final leg of the mission. Another black mark on the copybook.

I don't think I knowingly felt the pressure of holding the captain's role on the brink of a three in-a-row but perhaps I worried that history might repeat itself. And maybe I hinted at that fear while talking to Aoife about it at home.

But this does feel different compared to the last time I had this opportunity in 2007.

I'm a bit older, and at a more mature stage of my hurling career. It's a different group of players too. A different generation of athletes with different mindsets and outlooks on life. There are no groups or cliques. For that reason, this is probably the best group of players that I have shared a dressing-room with.

We weren't that far off getting over that line, and we were probably around 95 percent towards being in the right condition. For whatever reason, we fell short of the 100 percent mark. There's a five percent effort that has not been accounted for.

Maybe our appetite levels weren't where we thought they were. You need more firepower if you want to finish the three in-a-row job. The standard needs to be where it has been for the last two years... and higher.

You can't have anyone make a slip.

But it happened to us in 2007 and now, with me holding the captaincy role for the second time, we've fumbled our chance at history again in 2019.

*****

ST FINBARR'S IS a famously successful dual club. Also known as the Blues, we are the only club in the country to win All-Ireland senior titles in both men's football and hurling. A lot of GAA greats have been produced here, including Cork hurling and football legend... Jimmy Barry Murphy.

The Barr's is also home to the famous Meyler family. John Meyler won an All-Ireland medal with the Cork hurlers in 1986 and has built an impressive coaching CV, which includes terms in charge of the Wexford and Cork hurlers. Plenty of sporting legends have roamed these halls but our camogie team has yet to make a major imprint on the history here. We want our name on the roll of honour.

We have a massive sporting complex here, which was officially opened in 1970. The Barr's camogie club folded in the 1960s, but reformed in '72. But since the reformation, St Finbarr's has never won a Senior Camogie Championship title in Cork. Our goal is to change that.

IT'S 2006 AND the great Gerald McCarthy, also of Barr's blood, is in charge of our senior team. He has a backroom team which includes fellow Barr's man Bill O'Connell, who works in the navy and is just an all-round gas character. My mother Geraldine is involved too on the club committee. Mam has completely immersed herself in the club since the day she brought me here for my first introduction to the Barr's.

She's still a proud product of the Glen, but she helps out wherever she can here, from working on committees to coaching the underage teams, and helping to breed the next generation of Blues' talent.

Having someone like Gerald McCarthy coming on board with us is a huge boost. He's such an iconic figure in Cork, and in the Barr's as well. We're so close to making that breakthrough and Gerald, with all his hurling knowledge and managerial nous, is the extra component that we need to drive on. We won the Cork senior B title in 2001, but we know that this squad is made of more.

There's no secret sauce and we're aware of that, but we're right on the precipice of outright success and Gerald will give us an edge to our game that we've been missing. You feel like you have an extra shield on your back when you have someone of his status on the line, and in your corner. He has done it all.

As a player, he's one of the most decorated people in hurling history. He's a two-time All-Ireland winner with the Barr's and has won five All-Ireland medals with Cork, including a three in-a-row from 1976 to '78. In 1966, when he was the captain of both the Cork senior hurlers and Cork under-21 teams, he became the first player in GAA history to skipper two All-Ireland-winning teams in the same season. He has served as chairman of the Barr's in the past, and has had a successful management career so far too.

Alongside the iconic 'Canon' Michael O'Brien, he guided the Cork hurlers to All-Ireland success in 1990. That was an historic year for the county, as the Cork footballers also emerged as All-Ireland champions. That dual triumph has been given the immortal title of 'The Double'.

It's clear from the word go that Gerald wants to add to his managerial CV with us. We've tried to acquire his services many times before, but he was never available due to his commitments with other hurling teams. He has promised us for years that he would get involved, and he's taking the helm this year for one year only. But he's not here to just get through the season, tick the box and move on to bigger and better things.

He holds a meeting with us at the start of the year where he outlines his vision for the 2006 season. He has only one plan for us... to finish the year as county champions. Training under Gerald is great... very practical and very simple. Our set-up is excellent this year and every decision he makes is working for us.

Some of our more experienced players are coming to the end of their playing career. Former Cork player Colette O'Mahony is in her 21st year of loyal service to the Barr's, and is still waiting on that elusive senior county medal. Technically, she's already retired but Gerald has convinced her to come back into the breach once more.

We have a strong team and Colette, who is a brilliant free-taker, is a major part of that, so it's vital that she's here. There's a strong mix of young and old players in our squad. Ellen Clifford, Jenny Duffy and Viv Harris are All-Ireland winners with Cork, but more importantly... they're club players for the Barr's. Viv is a brilliant kickboxer who has represented Ireland in that sport, and is super athletic. Lynda O'Connell, who also hurls for Cork, is our captain.

There's so much potential in this group and we just need to unlock it.

WE'VE REACHED THE county final and we're up against Imokilly, which is a divisional team based in the east of Cork. Divisional sides are not something that you see in a lot of counties but they are an essential part of the Cork GAA fabric. Our county is of such a vast size that junior and intermediate clubs are separated into divisions based on the region in which they are located, and internal competitions are organised for each division.

They can then combine to compete in the Cork Senior Championship. The West Cork clubs are represented by Carbery, while the Cork city clubs play for Seandún. There's Avondhu for the North Cork clubs, and Carrigdhoun covers the region of South East Cork. Our county final opponents Imokilly represents the intermediate and junior clubs in East Cork.

Some brilliant Cork camogie stars play for Imokilly, including Mary O'Connor, Angela Walsh and Orla Cotter. There's lots of firepower in that squad to match anything we have. Either one of us could snag this.

Imokilly have scored 6-59 in their four championship games of this campaign, while we have banked 5-49. We defeat the reigning champions Cloughduv in the first round and pick up further wins against Kilbrittain, Aghabullogue and Muskerry to assure us of a place in the final.

Gerald's plan is coming together nicely. There's a lot of history on the line for our own team, and the wider St Finbarr's club. Our camogie team has never won a senior county title, and the Barr's has gone 13 years without a senior championship title. It's a wet and miserable October day when we meet Imokilly in the showpiece at Páirc Uí Rinn, and it's our opponents who make the brighter start by dominating the possession.

But they can't convert that superiority with points on the board. We survive that early storm and gradually grow into the contest before ultimately taking control of the tie.

A crucial two-minute period in the first-half gives us the platform to build our charge for victory. First up is a penalty awarded to us over a foul on Colette O'Mahony, which I convert. We get another goal through Rachel Myers after she pounced to block down an attempted clearance in the Imokilly defence.

We're in complete control now.

That sequence pushes us into a five-point lead at half-time and, ultimately, amounts to a three-point victory at full-time.

We now have our own place in the Barr's distinguished history. Our name is finally up there on the club's Mount Rushmore. Colette O'Mahony, whose frees were crucial to our win in the final, can now retire in peace with a deserved reward that she has waited two decades to receive. It's the ultimate send-off for such a valued member of our club who is held in such high regard.

The additional honour of being the team that brings back some Senior Championship silverware to the Barr's after a 13-year wait is another lovely achievement to savour. It's nice to have a city team winning the county title too, and it's great to reach such a milestone alongside your friends and the people that you've grown up with.

We reach the county final again the following year, and once more in 2008. But there's no three in-a-row beside our name in the Cork camogie archives. Gerald McCarthy has stepped down as manager and is now in charge of the Cork senior hurlers and has been replaced by a management ticket of Jerry Murphy and Ivan O'Mahony. In 2007, Muskerry dethrone us after a low-scoring final to capture their first senior county camogie crown in 74 years. Muskerry is another one of the divisional outfits, which mainly covers the junior and intermediate clubs in the Mid-Cork area. We get a chance to avenge that hurt in the 2008 decider, but again, we come up against a club that's aiming to end a title drought.

There's been a change in management again as Gerald McCarthy's son Derek steps in to take over. Douglas, which has the great Mackey sisters Katrina and Pamela on their player roster, beat us by 10 points in the final to win the Senior Championship for the first time in their club's history. Three consecutive county finals, with a return of just one success.

That's not a record that I ever wanted for my club and it shouldn't have happened. I can't explain it either. A few players who were integral to our victory in 2006 have left the squad and we're now in the midst of a fierce transitional period.

A possible Munster title eludes us in 2006 too.

A week after dispatching Imokilly, we progress to the Munster semi-final where we square off with Clare champions Kilnamona. But the day we make our first appearance in the provincial championship is also our last, as Kilnamona turf us out.

Out on our ass, and in our own club grounds too.

Looking around after the final whistle, we can't comprehend how we lost this one. We're surrounded by silence and disbelief. We led from the first to the 57th minute… and now it's all over.

Kilnamona score 2-2 in 11 minutes to swipe the win from our grasp. We were leading by six points at one stage, only to crumble in the dying moments and throw it all away. I think we can mark this one down as the consequence of a lack of concentration and, perhaps ,too much time spent on the post-county final celebrations. But at least our 2006 county triumph is set in stone, and a county title is hard earned.

That's particularly true in Cork. The transitional period is hurting us a bit more as the years go on and we've suffered further setbacks since then. From ascending to a point where we can contest county finals almost yearly, we have now regressed to losing the first and second round of the championship.

Cork has one of the best county championships in the country because of the sheer volume of teams competing in it. There's a good balance in the competition with a new winner emerging almost every year to keep the standard high and ensure a wide spread of players on the Cork county team. That might not be the case in other counties where one club dominates the county championship for years, and is represented by about five or six players on the starting team for their county. Clubs in Cork don't really get that opportunity to command the camogie championship and that's probably what catches us a little bit in the period after winning the title in 2006.

We did reach two more county finals and we know we're not a bad team, but the standard is so ferocious that defending a title is almost impossible.

It's a fair competition overall. UCC have even entered teams in the past which is a great challenge for club teams to measure themselves against quality players from strong hurling counties. We were drawn against them once. They had a star-studded team, filled with players from camogie strongholds in Kilkenny and Tipperary. Looking out at the pitch before the game, I struggled to see how we could beat such a powerful team.

But we did, and it was a case of the bond of a club player trumping a collection of talented players who have come together on a temporary basis. Games like that demonstrate how difficult opportunities can galvanise a team.

✳

IN CORK, THE captain of the camogie team is determined by the outcome of the senior county championship. A representative of the winning side is chosen by management to lead the county team for the season ahead. I have an inkling about who the management team might be considering as captain for the 2007 season.

My clubmates Jenny Duffy and Lynda O'Connell are members of the Cork panel, but I'm also aware that I've been a starting player for this team since making my debut in 2002. My instincts are confirmed by a fellow Barr's woman, Marian McCarthy, who informs me that the club is putting my name forward to represent the Blues as the Cork captain.

To solidify the selection, the nomination for captain must go through the county board. I know that step has been completed because I get a call from our trainer, and my former Cork teammate, Fiona O'Driscoll to confirm the news. Becoming the captain of our county team has never been an obsession of mine. It's an afterthought, really.

My main focus has always been, and will always be, to go out and play to the best of my ability. But when you are an established player, and think that you have certain qualities that portray leadership, and decision-making, it is pleasing to see that recognised. There's a certain stamp of approval in earning the role of captaincy.

It's a mark of respect to the work I've put in to date. It's a huge honour, but it doesn't take over my mindset and make me overthink my responsibilities as captain. The qualities for this job come naturally to me and I don't need to put on any show in front of the squad.

Obviously, I have faults too. I'm maybe a bit too aggressive and a bit too passionate but, that all said, I'm just delighted to have the opportunity to officially lead from the front. Of course, everyone in the squad has a responsibility to take on an unofficial role of leadership and there are a lot of strong characters here who can deliver on that. Aoife Murray is here as well as the likes of Elaine Burke and Emer Dillon. Jenny O'Leary is another stalwart who, although quiet at times, knows when it's the right time to offer a few inspiring words to the group.

She's a constant option when I'm preparing to deliver the ball into our forwards. Good teams with the right sense of ambition will never rely on just the captain to speak. There are enough strong-minded people here who have the confidence to say something when it needs to be said.

John Cronin from the Cloughduv club is our manager. He was my first proper Cork manager who invited me in to attend those trials where I was picked for the minor county team. John is a gentleman but, equally, he's not afraid to give us a kick up the ass when some tough love is required. He loves the game, and probably knows the strengths and weaknesses of every player in the county at the moment.

He's an excellent coach with a lovely manner. He knows a lot about the game of camogie and has the respect of everyone who loves the sport in this county. And with Fiona O'Driscoll alongside him, it's a great combination of coaching ability.

CHAPTER 16

This is probably the most emotional final from a personal point of view that I'm ever after playing: number 1, for Cork, who I love playing for, and ultimately, for my mother. I wouldn't be playing only for her, and she's really ill at the moment. Every game, every waking moment, she's there, and unfortunately, she can't be here today. She is just an amazing woman and she's fighting so hard at the moment. And it's all down to her.

– Gemma O'Connor, *The Sunday Game*, 2015 All-Ireland camogie final

IT'S A FEW minutes after winning the 2015 All-Ireland final.

We've just gotten the better of Galway to win our second All-Ireland in-a-row, and I'm being interviewed by Joanne Cantwell from *The Sunday Game*. She's telling me that the crowd are chanting my name, and is asking me about the emotion that I'm feeling now that we've eclipsed the final whistle.

I don't know who knows what about my mam's health, and whatever I'm saying is purely instinctive. What comes out, comes out.

It feels weird to talk about her in this capacity, knowing where she is. I can normally spot her face up there. Even in the swarm of faces that fill Croke Park on All-Ireland final day, I can always find her in the crowd.

I'm so used to having my mam at games all year round. I always call her on the morning of an All-Ireland final... she'd be up in the hotel with all my aunts, ready for the road. I always see her before and after games. But I can't call her today.

She's not with my aunts in the hotel and her face is nowhere to be seen in the stands of Croke Park. I'm not even sure if she's in the right condition to watch the game.

I appreciate the opportunity to talk about her for a few minutes and acknowledge her part in my life. Just to say it openly. On camera, to the whole nation... for everyone to hear. People should know who she is because the work she has put into my career, and into the sport of camogie, is the stuff that people don't see. Behind the curtain and away from the limelight.

It's her endeavour that has moulded the player I've become and I want to recognise that here. I hope every single person watching this clip knows who she is now.

*****

IT'S THE START of the 2015 season and I'm talking to my mam about going back to training with Cork. I've taken some time off since winning the All-Ireland final, but a new season is starting up. I'm conflicted about what to do.

Sport is great and it can be a relieving outlet when you're going through a painful time. But I want to be here, looking after my mam instead of rushing off to training. It might just be better for me to concentrate on one thing, instead of trying to split my time between everything.

Mam lays it all out simply for me to get some clarity in my head.

'I don't want you to go training and play if you don't want to be there,' she tells me. 'I don't want you to do it if you feel you can't give the full commitment... or if you're exhausted. But I do want you to go and play because I love to watch you play.'

And that settles it. Not going back to play for Cork is no longer an option. That's not to say that the indifference towards camogie goes away entirely. There's still some back and forth going on in my head. I sometimes feel like this is a waste of time, and I can't help myself from questioning my decision to be here when my mam is sick at home.

It's hard to fully enjoy it when I know the suffering that she is going through. I'm trying to be serious about something that really isn't that important. It's human to feel resentful at a time like this, but I'm still trying because I know that's what she wants for me. Playing camogie is the best thing I can do to make all of this a little bit easier on her. It makes her happy knowing that I'm here.

And even if I'm not enjoying this, it's enough to know that she's getting some comfort from me being here.

And if I didn't go, what would I be doing instead? Obviously, I'd be at home with my mam and caring for her. But what else?

Would I start eating badly? Drinking badly? I don't know, and that's the other side of the dilemma. A situation like this with a lot of heavy emotions involved can make you do foolish things. I could start going to bed, and not want to get up and go to work in the morning. Bad habits could sneak in while drastically changing my routine and that's the last thing my mam needs right now.

Sport is a big help for me too because exercise allows me to release different emotions and endorphins that keep me somewhat sane, and a little bit on the happy side. Even if it's only a tiny bit of relief at a time.

*****

MAM ISN'T REALLY religious, but throughout her illness, she's been trying to get in tune with a spiritual power that she doesn't really understand. Something a little bit bigger than this world and its forces… whether it's God or Jesus or some form of higher power. People give her holy medals from time to time and she takes solace from them.

Little tokens of hope.

She has miraculous medals for Glenn and myself to keep too. I wear it every time I play camogie. Any time I go to training or to a match, I always have my medal on, wrapped around the inside of my sports bra over my heart.

Always. By now, I've accepted that mam is sick, but I can't process anything more than that. Her future still seems uncertain to me.

Since going back on the treatment, mam has started losing her hair again. The hope was that her brother John would be styling her hair, but now he's going to be cutting it off. It's probably hard for both of them, but they're going to shave all of her hair off before she loses it entirely. It's the one thing she can do to steal back some of the control when everything else seems so inevitable.

Mam and I have the same eyebrow shape and I was afraid that she was going to lose them as well. She has beautiful eyelashes too. But it's at least some small mercy that they've stayed put for her.

*****

MY PHONE STARTS ringing one evening.

It's mam.

For the last while, a palliative care team and a community nurse have been calling to the house to help her with her treatment. They come out to help her self-inject, and to check up on her, especially if she's feeling quite unwell. They've told her that they think she should be admitted to Marymount Hospice in Cork, just to get her meds right and get the pain under control.

But the problem with Marymount is that you don't go in there to come back home.

'What, you're going to Marymount?' I say to her when she tells me about the suggestion over the phone.

'Yeah, it's only temporary. They said I'll be home at the weekend. What do you think about that?'

'I don't really want you to go to Marymount because of the place that it is.'

'But it's just temporary. It's just to get my pain under control.'

'Grand, I'll take you there, so!'

I head up to Ballyphehane while mam packs her bags. Dad and I are going to drive in with her. She sits into the front seat beside me, and dad gets into the back. As we reverse out from the house, I look over at her for a second.

She throws her gaze up towards the house and just shakes her head as she looks up at our home.

*****

IT'S ALL-IRELAND FINAL day and I'm having the same debate again. The same one I had last year, with all the same emotions racing around after each other in my head. It's the most important game of my life but it feels so minor all at once.

How can it mean anything more than that to me, when mam… who has given her whole life to make me the player that I am, can't be here because she's in a hospice with stage four cancer? I have to remind myself that this is all for her. Even if she's not well enough to watch the game on TV, I know she's here in another way.

She's aware in some way. Her medal is on my heart. Always. The whole weekend is like something out of the twilight zone. But I know what I have to do… win for her, and win for Cork. I just want to get out there and get the job done.

And after that, just get back to my mam.

Galway are our opponents today and their style of play always suits us. We both like to play an open game of camogie. It's not the same as when we play against a team like Kilkenny, where it's a lot more congested, dogged and there's not as much room to play. I certainly feel a bit freer playing this game.

I'm marking Niamh McGrath and she's sitting off the '45', not contesting a whole pile of possession with me. That's exactly the kind of game I want. It works for me because it means she's not causing any interference, and I can clean up anything that comes in. Julia White is doing a ferocious amount of work at midfield and Orla Cotter is in similar industrious form at half-forward. Orla Cronin and Amy O'Connor, two young stars with a bit of green around their ears, are putting in a monstrous shift in the forwards.

We're just a level or two above Galway, and we win by seven points.

We just bring a mentality and intensity that chokes Galway out. I think we're just a hair ahead of them now. But this Galway team is developing into a strong outfit and I think there's more to come from them. They're just a step behind ourselves and Kilkenny right now.

But I can sense that they're not far off making a breakthrough.

*****

MAM HAS BEEN in the hospice for a few weeks at this stage, and the cancer has now spread from her lungs and liver and into her brain. It's the day after winning the All-Ireland final, and I'm back in Marymount for a visit after spending last night in Dublin. Mam knows that we won, but she's not buzzing about the result.

There's no stir from her in the bed.

I'll never fully understand what mam knew or didn't know about her health. Or what she even admitted to herself. Maybe she suspected more about the pain in her back than what she spoke about it to me. I remember picking up on a strange vibe one time when she was sitting in a waiting room for an appointment. She loves cheeseburgers from McDonald's and I offered to go and buy her one before going in, but she didn't want one.

Maybe she just didn't have an appetite for one? Maybe her fears were so overwhelming that she couldn't stomach any food?

Maybe she really believed that going to Marymount would be a temporary arrangement? Maybe she always knew her chances were low, and she told me about the plan to just stay until the weekend to ease me into the reality of what's coming?

There are depths to her that I will never know.

There comes a time, in the course of every serious illness, when a conversation must happen. A proper talk to confront the reality of where you're at... and what's coming. Oncologists are fluent in this kind of language, and they always address patients bluntly. Oncologists in a hospice aren't really doctors. Their specialist training in this area of medicine is so precise that they can only deal in black and white when talking to you about what's going on in your body. They use the same approach when speaking to the families and the kids.

Sensitivities are for the family and friends of the patient. But at some point, your parents must take an example from the oncologists. It's her first week in Marymount and mam and I are having a coffee. She's wearing her housecoat while we chat.

This isn't a regular chat.

This one is a real talk.

'YOU'LL BE FINE without me,' she tells me.

It's the first time we've spoken about what's about to happen. Our first proper conversation and every word is painful to hear.

Now I know for certain that she knew what was ahead of her when she went into Marymount. You don't go into Marymount to really come back out.

This is a hospice.

Some people go in here for respite care, but she knew when she was going in, that she was probably never coming home again. That shake of her head, on the day we left Ballyphehane, was her last salute to the home house.

Dr Con Murphy's sister Marie is a palliative care consultant at Marymount.

She's a very straight up person… very direct. One of my aunts told me that she had a similar talk with my mam, and maybe mam took her cue from that to explain her situation to me.

She's helping me to prepare as we drink a cup of coffee.

She obviously felt that this was the right time to say it out to me.

*****

IT'S A SUNDAY and I've just heard that my cousin Gillian has died by suicide. Her body was found in the River Lee.

I had a club game with St Finbarr's today, and was just packing my bags to go and stay with mam at Marymount when I got the phone call from my aunt about the tragedy.

'We can't tell her!' she says, advising me not to give mam any more pain.

'It would just finish her!' My dad stayed with mam on the Sunday.

I head back into Marymount on Monday and mam is drifting into a deep sleep. Our family gets a call to come into the hospice, and by Thursday, I can tell that it's close.

It's the same day as my cousin's funeral.

I went to the removal and the rosary, and we agree that Glenn and dad should go to the funeral. I'm staying here at mam's bedside in Marymount, along with Aoife, and my aunt Francis.

I call Glenn and dad to tell them to come back… I know it's coming soon.

The human condition has an amazing, immeasurable ability, and I think I've always believed in that. Our family isn't religious. Not in the conventional sense anyway. Mam always lived by the moral code of living a good life, being a good person and doing good things. That was her religion.

Her church of worship.

But whatever powerful spirit is out there, something touched my mam that evening. Maybe the miraculous medal, and the faith she poured into it, had something to do with it. Whatever happened, as Glenn and my dad came in the door, my mam took her last few breaths.

It was about half past five.

Even the doctors, with all they know about the human body, can't explain why it happened that way.

Some things can't be explained by religion, or science… or anything else.

*****

THE FEW DAYS around mam's funeral have been so surreal, but at the same time, they keep you occupied from your grief. There's great power in numbers and we're blessed to be surrounded by our family and friends.

They help to ease the pain for that moment or that period of time when your mind wants to give in to darker thoughts. But you can't escape the bereavement forever. When you go home that night and the funeral is over, that's when it really hits you.

They're gone and they're not coming back.

I'm staying in Ballyphehane tonight, in my old room where mam slept.

She moved in here while she was sick. Aoife and my cousin Alison are staying over as well. Alison is a tall monster of a woman, standing up strong at about 6' 2". We always stayed in each other's houses while we were growing up and she's one year younger than me.

She asks if she can sleep with Aoife and myself tonight.

'That's my memory of your mam,' she says.

I suppose she just wants to be close. That's when I realise how far grief can stretch when a loved one dies. Obviously, you're so hurt from losing a parent, but everybody has lost someone. My mam was a sister, a best friend, an aunt and a daughter to somebody. My poor nan is still alive at almost 90 and she has just endured a pain that no parent should ever have to bear. She can't wrap her head around my mam's death.

To lose a daughter at that age is incomprehensible. Dad just says nothing... he's struggling to express what he feels. Quiet and subdued appear to me to be his default reactions in tough circumstances. You can never get over the loss of your wife, but I don't think he has come to terms with it either.

We don't do anything with him at Christmas, because he doesn't want to do anything without her during the holidays. Glenn and myself spend the day at my aunt's house. I collect him in the morning and we normally do a Christmas swim for charity and make a donation to either Marymount or cancer research.

We have breakfast at mine and then go up to my aunt's house in the evening. Dad spends the day by himself. I prepare his dinner the night before and drop it out to him on Christmas morning. That's just how he wants to spend his Christmas Day.

He just waits for the day to pass… and it's over before you know it.

Whether you're religious or not, Christmas Day is a sacred event that should be spent in the company of your family. But that's not what my dad wants without mam. I can't do anything about that. If that's what he wants to do with his days from here on in until the day he dies, then that's his decision. That's how he copes.

He has his new routine without my mam and he likes it that way. I sometimes make suggestions that he should do something else, or I might invite him to come out for a walk with us, but he's not interested in any new adventures.

My mam is buried in Rathcooney cemetery, which is close to where her family is from on the northside of the city. It's where my grandad is buried, as is my nan, who has since passed away. When I was younger, mam always joked about where to bury her if she ever died.

'Promise me, whatever happens to me… you won't send me to St Joseph's!' she'd say, messing with me. St Joseph's cemetery in Ballyphehane is one of the oldest cemeteries in Cork and my dad has a plot there. But after my mam passed away, my uncle Michael made a suggestion to dad about where to lay her to rest.

'You took her away from her own people on the northside. I think you need to send her back now!'

My dad visits her grave every Sunday even though he lives a bit further away from the cemetery. I'm a bit closer to the graveyard, and I used to visit mam's grave a lot.

I still try to call in when I can, but I probably don't go that often anymore. Glenn doesn't go at all because he just doesn't like going up there. My aunts don't really go either, apart from on her birthday or at Christmas time.

I think back to that day in July, when mam and myself took Molly out to the Regional Park for a walk and a puckaround. You couldn't identify her as a sick person that day, and yet her condition deteriorated so rapidly in the months after. She was pucking the ball around in the summer… and died in September.

How can someone's health regress so much in the space of a few weeks? Some questions around my mam's illness can't be answered. Another inexplicable detail of an inexplicable chapter in my life.

I always wear mam's wedding ring as a chain and habitually put my hand on my chest to check that it's still there. One day, while I was out meeting someone for a coffee, the chain broke and I couldn't feel the ring.

I was a lunatic for a second, panicking that it might have vanished. Rings are so small, easy to lose, and a nightmare to find. My heart just sank. But the ring had actually just dropped down between my sports bra and my t-shirt.

In Cork, we refer to moments of good luck as being 'haunted'.

And I was definitely haunted that day. Mam's hand caught it for me. When Aoife and I got married, I left mam's ring off and wore a locket that Aoife gave to me. It had pictures of my mam and my nan inside for the bouquet.

There is so much of mam's memory that I'll keep forever.

I still have one of the bandanas she wore while she was sick. Her miraculous medal is with me too. Her heart on my heart.

Always.

PART SIX

LET YOU BE YOU

Gemma gets her kit and equipment ready (top) before a 15k loaded walk during recruitment training, and (left) celebrating her passing out parade in Collins Barracks with her brother Glenn and fellow recruit Carmel Bennett

A farewell from family before UN duty, where Gemma enjoyed comradeship and the occasional puck-around far from home.

CHAPTER 17

IT'S HOLIDAY TIME for Aoife and myself, and this is an important vacation. We go to Lanzarote for 10 days and I try several times to get the words out. The original plan is to ask on day three... but we're on day five, and I still can't muster the courage. I'm trying my best not to say anything too cringey, but I have to get the question out.

We both have this inside joke that every time we go to Lanzarote, Aoife always suggests getting bikes and I'm allergic to that. I hate getting bikes and cycling around the place. So, this time, I ask if we should get bikes?

We always cycle out to Playa Honda, where the Spanish go on holidays. We stop to take a break and sit down. By now, I'm like a cowering child and Aoife senses what is about to happen. She's toying with me like she's playing with the last of the food on her dinner plate.

The massive u-turn on the bikes thing is probably what gave me away.

'Are you going to look at me?' she asks, urging me to get on with it and ask the question. It's funny because I wouldn't really get embarrassed easily, or afraid.

But this is a different kind of question.

I tell dad, my aunts and Glenn about my plans before heading off on holiday. Eventually, I relieve us both of the horrible tension and get the big question out. She's delighted to agree. We head off for drinks and dinner that night before announcing our engagement to our families.

WHEN I THINK about weddings, none of the traditional rituals appeal to me. The white wedding convention is just not my fit. I don't want all that attention. Put me in front of thousands of people with a hurley in my hand and a jersey on my back. Now, that's comfort to me. No stage fright there.

But I just can't imagine all those people looking at me walking down the aisle. Originally, we wanted to invite 180 guests, but Covid-19 restrictions force us to whittle it down to 50. Even 50 people looking at me as a bride is too many. I confide in Aoife that I'm going to be embarrassed on what is supposed to be the happiest day of my life. But then we get into it and design our wedding to our liking.

We have total control to customise everything, and that puts me at ease. Aoife takes care of most of the organising, and starts making the connections. Vendors, photographers, videographers, the music... it all starts slotting into place.

We choose Dromquinna Manor in Kerry as our venue.

As we get into it, I start to get a bit more comfortable with the process. The guy that made my dress was amazing. He just made the whole experience so easy, and so fun. I go with pants, a top, and an overskirt. My aunt gives me the heels that she wore to her own wedding. Neither the overskirt nor the heels last the whole night.

The overskirt comes off first while we're on the dance floor. My cousin, who is a bit tapped, is egging me on... 'Errrra, take it off!' she says, as everyone is having a great time. It falls into the hands of my aunt, who snatches it in the air like she's catching a bouquet. She then throws it up on her head before coming out to dance.

The heels came off after another hour and I put on the runners. I tell my brother Glenn that he can say a few words during the afters, and in his speech he tells our guests about what he learned from having an older sister. I gave him the gift of the example of what not to do. He tells them all about a time that I got caught committing the mortal sin of underage drinking. And, yes, I will confess to a bit of sneaky drinking in my time.

Say your prayers for my damned soul!

And of course, he was lurking in the background, taking notes on my erroneous ways. All pretty harmless stuff, but I suppose it does make for good wedding speech material.

Everyone is having a ball and it's exactly the kind of day I wanted from the minute I asked Aoife to be my wife. The result of the 2015 referendum means it's a solid, legal union too. It feels more as if there's 150 guests here, with all the craic that's filling the room. I would love to have been able to invite all of my camogie comrades here but the Covid rules won't allow it today. Fifty is the limit, and we have no choice but to scale the whole event back.

Aoife Murray is here though. After all our years of running the line together, she's an easy inclusion in our wedding guest list. A day I thought I would dread ends up being a day I would love to repeat. It's such an intimate occasion with just our own. It all works out perfectly.

Our wedding is a spiritual ceremony, and our celebrant, Carol Cotter, is a neighbour of my mam's. The two of them grew up together. We decline the offer to write our own vows and just each submit a story, which Carol uses in the ceremony. My dad is quite emotional on the morning of the wedding. He feels lonely without mam when he's going to places and doing things like this.

But she is there, in a different way.

I see some of her in Aoife. I have a running joke with her about a weird habit mam had that's manifesting through my wife now. If mam bought something to cook and I told her that I liked it, she would buy it forever more for me. She'd always have it on the O'Connor menu.

And now, with Aoife, she does the same thing.

I would be laughing, saying, 'Just because I said I liked it, doesn't mean I want to eat it 70 times in-a-row'. A bit repetitive perhaps, but all they're doing is trying to make me happy. They clicked straightaway when Aoife started coming to Ballyphehane.

Mam was a bit of a messer and a bit of a child with Peter Pan syndrome. She just loved the craic, much like all my aunts. They loved each other's company and enjoyed each other's silly humour.

MAM IS INVOLVED in our wedding day too.

We use her scarf for a hand-fastening ceremony.

We include Aoife's nan in the ceremony as well, who has also passed away. She's a real gaeilgeoir, so we have Sean-nós music on the day.

Aoife has a lovely Celtic coin belonging to her too and she puts that on her bouquet. Neither of us really had a hen party. We just headed back down to West Cork, to Heir Island for a weekend and a kind of mini-hen.

It's nice to go back to where we shared that evening of cheese, crackers and wine in 2012. Where it all started.

*****

IT'S 2015, AND Ireland has just become the first country to legalise same-sex marriage after a referendum. It's an historic event… such a unifying moment.

People have flown home to Ireland just to vote and do everything they can to ensure the result goes our way. The Yes vote prevails by 62 percent to 38 percent. That's 1.2 million people who agree that I should have the same marital rights as a heterosexual person.

It's a resounding win for equality.

Aoife plays a massive role in achieving that result after going around door-to-door to canvas for the Yes vote. My uncles and her friends play their part in that too, including some of her straight friends, which is such a lovely act of solidarity. With work and camogie taking up so much of my time, I'm not in a position to volunteer.

They have a few unfortunate encounters with people waving their No stickers on the campaign trail. Some of it's kind of funny, and we'd be laughing at them saying, 'Oh, I'm not voting for that. Get away from my door. It's an abomination… it's disgusting!'

The result is such a special moment for us.

It's so heartening the way the whole country unites for liberty. For everyone. The majority of the country wants us to have the same rights and opportunities as everyone else. They're saying that they support us to live truthfully and happily.

Unfortunately, I'm training on the day of the result. You get so wrapped up in that world of playing and training, and thinking about games. Everything else becomes less of a priority and that's not really realistic or sustainable. It affects your whole life and you miss out on so much. For example, I've never attended the Pride festival.

I've actually been to very few events in my life, in terms of gigs or concerts. I just don't think I was ever really available to do any of those things.

When you're playing at county level, camogie is your priority. The everyday things in life are secondary to that, meaning there's not much time for events like Pride, which is something that I should support. And sometimes Pride is an organised event for people who run in the same circle, whereas our circle is camogie players and ladies footballers. I don't get to socialise in pubs very much, but when I do it's mainly in straight bars and the occasional gay bars. But Pride is a celebration and it's something I hope to experience in the future.

Don't get me wrong, you gain so much from representing your county, but you do miss out on important things. That's the unfortunate trade-off. Hindsight is a great thing but when you look back on it, you wonder how you even maintain that commitment for so long? You start to become paranoid that you're draining everyone around you with too much talk about the game. I sometimes try to direct conversations towards some other topic… worrying that people might think I have no other interests in my life.

Playing sport at that level is one big sacrifice.

Anyone that tells you otherwise is talking a load of bullshit. Of course you love the game and all the cliches that go with it, but is the constant cycle of training and games a pain in my arse sometimes? Of course it is. There are times when I don't want to be there at all. That's reality. There's no player… male or female, that can convince me they love going out training 24/7… four days a week.

Getting up training at eight o'clock on Saturday and Sunday morning… for years on end? You would have to be sadistic to enjoy anything about that.

It's human to feel that way.

Winning an All-Ireland is the ultimate reward, but the workload involved in reaching that goal takes so much from you. You have very little down-time and your partner and your family lose out because of your absence. It's a completely selfish world. Of course, you enjoy it, but there are times when you don't, and there's nothing wrong with that.

You don't have to turn in your gear over a completely understandable reaction to the punishing sides of sport.

I think people get misled by this idea of being the perfect GAA player… giving the perfect quotes to the media, and fitting the perfect profile. People often forget that we're not professionals. We're people and workers first, and sports people after that.

It's a pain in the ass when you have a s**t day at work and then you're just expected to bury that emotion to be all fecking happy and motivated on the pitch.

GAA players don't have the resources or privileges that the professional athletes enjoy. You don't get up and have a five-star breakfast the morning after a match. You don't have everything looked after for you. You don't get to do your rehab in the morning, go for a swim and then do your weights and pitch sessions.

You're heading off to work, or school or college, and trying to fit all your training in around that. I think people sometimes portray an image which suggests that we have access to those things, but we simply don't. So, when you immerse yourself in that world, big occasions like the result of the marriage referendum tend to pass you by.

*****

I'VE ALWAYS TRIED to normalise my relationships.

That's just the way I have always approached it. I don't want it to be a big issue or a big deal because, to me, it isn't. This is just the person I'm with… and this is them and this is me. I'm not big into waving rainbow flags behind me or listening to Pink 24-7 but I just try to make it as normal as possible.

It's funny watching people try not to be awkward about it, and doing their absolute best to show you how progressive they are. We meet people in the local parish and they'd be going… 'That's Gemma now, and her paaaartner!'

It's almost like a code to subliminally let others know that there's a gay couple in the area. RED ALERT! RED ALERT! My friends and I always thought it was funny when people said it. We would be laughing, putting on a funny voice and going, 'Oooh, this is my paaartner'… and 'Don't say girlfriend!'

I think the term came from the older generation.

I hear heterosexual people saying partner more and more these days. Older couples who aren't married say partner too. I never stick rigidly to any one way of informing people about my relationship. I say partner, I say girlfriend… and now, I get to call Aoife my wife, which is very weird to me.

A very formal label.

There's no stereotypical gay person, but I suppose years ago, people always saw gay women as either sporty or tomboyish.

Aoife's quite the opposite. People might find it harder to place a label on her, and that's why I don't necessarily like labels... you just like who you like!

The sexuality spectrum is so diverse and fluid. It's a complete minefield and you could talk about it all day. There are so many identities and preferences, I can't even keep up with what's happening now. Gay, straight, bisexual, pansexual... it's a long list of orientations and of all the labels that are currently there, you might not even find anything that completely captures who you are.

Humans are evolving all the time. But whether you pin yourself to a label or not, I do think people are capable of falling in love with people, whether that's a man or a woman, or same sex. I suppose that's what happened with us.

There's no description to capture who we are, and we just happened to find happiness with each other.

It's important not to box yourself off from your desires. You don't know anything if you don't try it. You might think you're completely straight and that you'd never fall for a woman, but until you meet somebody, you're not really going to know that.

And if, God forbid... it didn't work out with me and Aoife, who's to say she wouldn't meet another man... or a woman? I don't know.

The same applies to me. I can still see an attraction in men, and I don't believe that you are just shut off from one gender because you find love elsewhere. You can't control what makes you happy.

That's just life.

I'VE KNOWN WHO I am from the moment I could think.

From very early on, I can sense there's something different about what I'm attracted to. There's no period of self-denial and I never feel like I should repress how I feel or stay in the closet, as the saying goes. That's not to say that I'm only interested in women from the word go.

It's not like that's really an option because that's not what society pushes you towards as you grow up. I was with boys before I was with women, and I always gave myself a chance to explore.

I GO TO the underage disco at a local hockey club in Harlequins and start heading for nightclubs in town once I reach around fifth or sixth year in secondary school. Throughout that time, I'm just experiencng the opposite sex, like everybody else.

But I always felt the other feeling was stronger. I was always attracted to women more than men. It was just something that was part of me, and I never felt that it was this overwhelming thing that took over and this is all people think of… or this is all of who I am.

This is who I am… I play camogie… I'm in the army… and I have a wife.

That's all you really need to know about me.

My sexuality is just one part of my life. But it hasn't always been easy. It isn't easy for anyone who belongs to the LGBTQ+ community. One of my uncles on my mother's side is gay. He had his ear bitten off in a nightclub, basically, for being gay. I know a GAA player who is openly gay, and who was subjected to disgraceful abuse while playing in a league game against a rival ream.

This is why men are emotionally repressed and don't talk about things. Or come out. How can they when we don't create a safe environment for them to live authentically?

Don't get me wrong, some innocent mind-games are harmless. That's just trying to get inside the mind of an opponent and edge them out psychologically. But there's a difference between giving someone an elbow or telling a player that their manager is warming up another player to replace them… and calling someone a 'faggot'.

That's a whole different level of abuse.

THE GAA CULTURE is something that I don't like for that reason, and it's the same in soccer. These are games that are perceived as manly men playing manly hurling and football. You have to fit a certain profile for you to qualify as a man.

Verbal assaults at a football match is the reward they get for not hiding from themselves. Some way to treat someone who has the courage to not be a fraud. Knowing what could be waiting for them if they do take the step to come out… a gay man will worry that people will think less of them for it.

Maybe they're afraid to come out because they think it might create a weird atmosphere among their teammates in the shower after training and matches. It should be just widespread acceptance and support, but unfortunately, that's not always the case. There's the whole sordid pub culture that goes with it too, which makes it all the more difficult for people to be brave and find peace in their identity.

In my opinion, it's harder for male players to come out, compared to female players, but it's no picnic for women either.

Kelly Holmes, the two-time Olympic champion for Great Britain, recently announced in public that she is gay. Her family has known for a long time but this was her first time to tell the world about who she is. I remember watching Kelly all the time during her running career. She's known since she was 17, but to speak openly about her sexuality at 52 must be daunting for her.

It's life-changing to come out and talk about your sexuality at that age. I saw her talking about it on the TV show *This Morning* and you can tell that she's nervous as she speaks her truth. That's probably because she could never do it when she was younger. Maybe it was due to her job as an army officer that she held back on that aspect of her life. Or perhaps she was worried about how it might impact her athletics career.

But to finally say it out loud at that stage of your life must be pretty scary. Especially when you have an iconic status like Kelly Holmes.

It's different for me because I'm comfortable with talking about it. Everyone has known the truth about my sexuality since I was young. For me, it's easy to talk about it, but for people at a more advanced stage in their life, it must be pretty scary.

*****

I'M OUT IN Cork city one night when a friend of mine rings me in distress. She's getting harassed and things are kicking off outside a bar. I'm just about to get into a taxi when she phones to tell me that a guy is calling her names over her sexuality.

When I arrive, I see that her aggressor is about 6' 7" and standing in a doorway while she's crying. He starts pushing me when I question him about it, and then I boot him up the ass to protect my friend. I later find out that this guy actually works in Cork and I see him all the time. He was hassling her because she's gay.

Things can go horribly wrong in seconds, but those incidents are 10 a penny. Unfortunately, you will always have people who will try to incite violence over nothing more than who you are.

On another night, I'm outside a bar when two lads roar out a comment from across the road. Not happy with what they've said, I decide to chase after them. One of them takes off, thinking I won't catch up, and I surprise them when I do.

I trip one of them up mid-chase, and he falls straight into the middle of the road just as a car is passing. I can't just tolerate the offence, but I also can't stop myself from thinking about what would have happened if he was struck by the car.

I believe that it's important to stand up for yourself but, sometimes, it can come at a cost. And instead of just walking away, you do stupid things.

*****

WOMEN IN SPORT are probably more in tune with their masculine side as well as their feminine side. Compared to male athletes, I think it's a little bit easier for women to have same-sex relationships, especially in our GAA world. The assumption is there's a lot more for women in sport to come out as gay.

And that's not just in the GAA community... it's in soccer, rugby and in all sports around the world.

As I go through my twenties, I discover that going to pubs and nightclubs can be a nightmare. People, mainly from the GAA community, talk to me, thinking they know me and that they can just say whatever they like. Some of the post-match chat is fine, it's game-specific. You go to certain pubs after games and people say, 'Congratulations, well done, Gemma!'

But then you have people whom you don't even know, coming up and saying, 'Oh, you're gay!' They just blurt out the most inappropriate remarks without even considering the impact that it could have on me.

Who the feck are you? I'm thinking to myself... *I don't even know you.*

The man who was harassing my friend that night is a big part of that unpleasant GAA pub scene community. It's a minority group but they are out there and they're not afraid to be loud about their ignorance.

Sometimes I bite back when they provoke me. That probably just typifies who I am... I wear my heart on my sleeve. But as time goes on, I learn to treat their homophobia with silence. Sometimes that's the only way to guarantee your peace.

AT HOME, MY mam says, 'I didn't know, but I wasn't shocked!'

As she has a brother who's gay, there's no issue there for her. Glenn just shrugs off the news and says, 'So what? She's still my sister.'

But for me, my dad is my cross to bear with my sexuality. He's difficult about some things in life and this is another thing that he can't understand. That's just him. I can deal with the people who disrespect me, but dad has been my biggest problem to face in terms of my sexuality.

He was there by my side on my wedding day, but honestly, I think he's still a bit funny about the whole thing. People might think that they're accepting of the LGBTQ+ community, but maybe it's more difficult to apply that when it's your own child who tells you they're homosexual.

The first few years after I get my status out in the open are particularly difficult at home. The underlying tension is my dad finding it hard to accept who I am.

It's only after I move out of the home house that we start to enjoy some calm again in the family. It's time to begin a new chapter in my life. We all just need some space if we are to work through this and reach an understanding.

My work with the army keeps me on the move too, so that's another motivation for me to leave the nest and find my way.

✶

IT'S JUST NOT always an easy road. Some families are way more accepting than others, and some people have completely different experiences. Your family might be really supportive but your friends might not be, or vice versa.

Some people might take a very long time to come out, and the struggle can be further complicated by depression, anxiety, and suicidal tendencies. It's crazy to think that people go through all that because of who they are, but that's why being comfortable with your identity is so important. And why it's equally important to surround yourself with people who accept, and love you for your identity.

You might face some, or a lot of opposition in your life, but you should never deny yourself from yourself. There's so much to enjoy when you give yourself permission to live sincerely.

That really rings true for me after our wedding.

One or two girls get in contact with me on Instagram with some really lovely messages. *Thank you for being you,* they write. *You've helped me with my sexuality.* That means so much to me.

That's just one or two people that I can do that for, and hopefully, it's just the start. I know I'm living right but messages like that are such a massive incentive to keep going, and influence others to do the same. It's great to know that people are seeing this as normal and that you can be who you want to be, without fear.

For anyone who is struggling with their identity or sexuality issues, there are a few things you need to understand. You can't run from yourself.

Your true self won't just disappear if you try to ignore it, or pretend it doesn't exist. You have to confront it and the first person you must admit it to is yourself. Once you've accepted you for you, it's important to try and talk to someone that you can trust.

That might be a family member, a teammate, a friend or maybe even a counsellor.

The best thing you can ever do is open up to someone you feel comfortable with, and talk about what's worrying you. That's obviously not a simple order to follow, especially if you live in a household with people who don't have an open or progressive mindset.

Maybe there's a parent who has a way of life that's discouraging to you. But even if there is a chance that you won't be accepted, you should still say it out loud.

At least then, it's out in the open and off your chest.

Carrying it around like a horrible secret is far more damaging to your mental health. It's exhausting to live in fear, worrying that someone might figure you out… every day. That can provoke people to have suicidal ideations, depression and anxiety. I know it's not easy, but you must do all you can to avoid creating a dangerous environment for yourself. And have some faith as well.

You might get a good response from your friends and family when you open up about something like this. But either way, you're unburdening yourself of something that your family should know.

Take that weight off your shoulders.

How can you live the life you're supposed to lead, if you're not true to yourself? You may have to lose some people along the way, but you'll find your tribe too. That might take some time but the journey to finding yourself is always easier than trying to live a lie.

But regardless of how people react to your news, try to remember that this is the most natural feeling to have and you haven't done anything wrong. You didn't murder anyone! It's crazy to feel that way, but it's just the way society treats homosexual people that these feelings of guilt or shame can often come up.

It seems so fickle in one sense, but it's also such a big thing all at once. But if you do encounter some difficulties with the reaction of others, there are so many services and support networks that can help you through it. If you're involved in the GAA, you can contact the Gaelic Players Association (GPA) and lean on their services.

The GPA is an excellent group who promote things like Pride month, and offer a safe space for LGBTQ+ members of the GAA. They also have counsellors that you can confide in, if you feel overwhelmed.

There's a new GAA club called Na Gaeil Aeracha which is Ireland's first LGBTQ+ inclusive gaelic games team. That's a great step forward too, and a brilliant outlet for anyone who feels isolated due to their sexuality. Of course, I'm always available to talk to anyone in the GAA community who needs my help with anything, and that includes issues around sexuality.

Creating a safer space for male GAA players to come out is a tough one to figure out, and change is coming very slowly, but initiatives like this help make it easier for them. I know the GAA referee David Gough said that he thought by coming out, it might pave the way for other male GAA players to follow suit. I'm sure the former Cork hurling goalkeeper Dónal Óg Cusack had similar hopes for the future after he revealed his sexuality to the public.

Really, it hasn't happened yet in gaelic games, but it has in rugby.

Leinster's Nick McCarthy recently came out to the public a few months after telling his teammates. It was such a powerful moment for men in Irish sport, especially after the mental torture he went through before telling everyone his truth. He said that he struggled to see a future in which he could play rugby as a gay man, and even considered retiring from the sport.

But he did take the brave step to trust his teammates and say what he needs to say to secure his future happiness. He's a brilliant example for anyone who is struggling to come to terms with who they are.

When I first started playing with the Cork seniors 19 years ago, it was all *hush, hush, giggle giggle*... and let's try to find out who all the gays are. There were a lot of nasty people behind that movement. The GAA is definitely going in the right direction with trying to address that but I just hope that it opens the door for more male players to come out.

The bottom line is to be honest with yourself and talk to somebody.

Try to deal with whatever situation arises, and just tackle it day by day. I really believe that Irish people are generally very accepting. There might be a few people in your life that might react unfavourably, but it's their loss at the end of the day.

Allow yourself to live the life that's meant for you.

Let you be you.

CHAPTER 18

IT'S THE 2007 ALL-IRELAND final and I'm about to experience my first bitter taste of being the captain of a Cork team that loses on the biggest day of the year. The old saying about goals winning games is on display here, as Wexford strike for the net twice between the third and 15th minute of the first-half.

Úna Leacy from the famous Oulart-The Ballagh club grabs both of the goals which ends up becoming the killer as Wexford prevail by two points. We clock up 11 wides too, seven of which occur in the first-half, which is far too high a number of missed chances. There's a last-minute goal chance for us to snatch the victory in the closing moments. Orla Cotter snakes her way through to get a shot off but her attempt comes back into play. I'm quickest to the rebound but I come away short changed too after my shot.

That's the last pang before the inevitable follows.

Wexford are walking away with the profits.

It's not the result we came here to achieve but I enjoyed performing the captain's role this year. And I thought the group was content within the set-up. However, that doesn't seem to be the case with everyone. But this information is only coming to my attention now, when it's too late to address the issues.

I feel a bit disillusioned because I thought things were good. I had a good relationship with John Cronin, our manager, and Fiona O'Driscoll, who is part of the backroom team. I thought my approach to the team was good and I thought we all worked well together. The word is that some people were unhappy with things this year, but nobody approached me at training to communicate the disquiet.

No one said, 'We need to fix this' or 'We need to talk about this' and without that, I couldn't take any action to help us confront the problems. And there's no point in having a bitch about something afterwards, when the opportunity to do anything about it has passed you by.

But from my perspective, I think there are some clique groups in the squad which are probably down to different personalities, people going to college together. I don't know, and it's hard to put a finger on it. People are naturally going to have good friends on a team and you might not necessarily be as friendly with everyone else.

I have noticed the presence of cliques in the Cork squad since about 2002, and in some years, that dynamic worked well for us because the talent was there to overshadow any personal differences. But then it's often the case that people will identify faults in a system when the season ends in defeat.

Perhaps, if we won, people might have considered the set-up to be perfect and nobody would have made any negative comments. Maybe people are looking to blame others for why we lost? Maybe they felt the set-up wasn't right?

I didn't see any evidence of unhappiness in the squad this year, but this is what was expressed to me in the aftermath.

*****

DISCORD CAN MANIFEST in different ways through a squad.

When Clare Shine broke into the panel in 2012, she noticed that some players weren't happy with her drifting in and out of the panel on account of her scheduling constraints. She discusses that period of her life in her excellent autobiography *Scoring Goals In The Dark.* She returned to the Cork squad in 2016 briefly, but left shortly after.

Paudie had told me that she was around and I sent her a text to encourage her to come back in for another go. I told her that we'd love to see her at training and that she would be a vital asset to the team. It's one thing to be asked by the manager, but if you don't feel welcomed by the girls, that's another issue. That's why I sent her the text... I genuinely wanted her to get involved.

And the 2016 bunch were a nice group to play with. Clare did return to training with us, but unfortunately, it didn't last. Those horrible pre-season track sessions probably broke her a bit. That's understandable and we're all breathing through our asses anyway. But I could tell that she was still coping with external issues relating to her mental health. You need a clear mind for that fitness work, and she probably couldn't concentrate with everything that was going on for her.

I never spoke to anyone in the 2012 panel who had an issue regarding the arrangement with Clare. But even if anyone did, their anger is misplaced. It's not Clare's fault that she's excelling in other sports. As long as she has something to offer to the squad, she deserves her place here. Paudie can identify the talent that she can bring to the table and he knows how to utilise her powers in our forward line. There will always be players whinging in a squad. You're dealing with over 30 players in a group where only 20 will be called into service during a championship game in either a starting or substitute capacity. And generally, it's the same players who consistently get the nod.

It's impossible to keep everyone satisfied, but I've never had a problem with having an open policy in a panel. The door is always off the latch for someone to come in and show what they can do. That's sport.

Players get called up, others get dropped and some might be late additions to the squad. If someone has a skillset that can benefit the team then I can't really see any other answer, other than to bring them in. Of course, that's a hard reality to accept when you're there training day in and day out, and you're already not getting much game time. The sight of a newcomer means you could get pushed even further out of contention to play.

But, again, that's the cruel side of sport. Sometimes, you have to make brutal calls as a manager, and the talent of one player outweighs the hours of commitment in another player. It sounds tough, but a good manager will have the courage to be a ruthless leader.

*****

I'M IN THE shop one day buying a few bits, and a woman I know through camogie is approaching me. I'm praying that she doesn't want to talk about sport but that's just wishful thinking. Not realising my relationship with Paudie, she proceeds to give out about him and I'm not sure what to say to her.

I don't bother responding with what I actually want to say. I just want to get away from her and there's no point getting confrontational with her because that's not an argument that I can win. With the way she's talking, she's certainly not going to listen to reason. There's a harsh reality of sport that some people don't want to face, and complaining about the situation is the only solution they can come up with.

Not everyone can play and there is only so much playing time that can be distributed among the panel. But they don't want to confront that and would prefer to lean into their own delusions.

Cork people have a conflicted relationship with their own.

Former Cork goalkeeper Dónal Óg Cusack came to speak to us once and he summed up the divisiveness in our county brilliantly… 'We're passionate, we're fiery, and we argue with ourselves'. He's essentially saying that we're eating ourselves from the inside out and he's completely correct. There are those who would love to see Cork falter over their own failed dreams. They have a chip on their shoulder and feel burned by the county team. They believe they were overlooked, or never got picked and maybe the sport didn't treat them kindly. I encounter so much of that every day.

People would come up to me and would have no bother pressing their opinion on me without a thought about how those remarks might affect me. I sympathise with the player who has been a substitute on a team for five or 10 years but, at the end of it all, you're the person that's making the decision to be part of the team. Nobody's forcing you to be here and, sometimes, you have to accept that there are other people out there who are just better than you.

There are times when I disagree with a manager's selection call, and would argue that one player deserves to start over another, but those decisions are for the manager only to make. Rightly or wrongly, there can only be one voice at the top. The players who feel neglected choose to focus on the begrudgery and the negativity. And then the disillusionment can prompt people to do stupid things.

I've witnessed occasions where the parents of adult players, at senior level, have tried to interfere on their child's behalf over issues related to playing time. That shouldn't even be tolerated at juvenile level, but it is unforgivable to see it at the adult grade. The manager is there in a voluntary capacity and the parent of a player – particularly a senior one – has no right to confront a manager like that to complain. These women are adults.

If my parents did that, I would have a fatal heart attack out of mortification, but some people are oblivious to their own behaviour. There is a time and place to air a person's grievances in a more appropriate way.

What bothers me the most is senior players articulating their frustrations in quiet circles instead of bringing it to the attention of the manager. They have little sneaky private conversations but don't have the stones to say it out loud. At least if you get it out there, we can try and work it out.

You can spot the groups in the corner who are pissed off. Just be an adult about it and have it out with the group. That kind of behaviour is what makes players like Clare Shine feel isolated and unwelcomed, when she should be receiving encouragement and support. But that's something that exists in pretty much every team. Someone is always going to be giving out when they're not getting their way.

*****

IT'S A HUGE regret for me that I never captained Cork to an All-Ireland title. I've had two opportunities and failed both times. It stings me all the more knowing that the two terms of my captaincy also coincided with the chance to win three in-row. Being the player that leads the troops up the steps, tired and satisfied from battle, is one thing, but that added layer of history would have been such an honour for me.

Unlike my 2007 experience, I wasn't selected as captain through the traditional route this time around. The Barr's didn't win the 2018 county championship, but Paudie wanted to appoint me as captain anyway. To make that happen, he appealed to the county board that he wanted to make a change and pick the captain himself from the entire squad.

Inniscarra were the 2018 camogie champions in Cork, defeating Courcey Rovers in the final to win their third successive title. By the existing law in the Cork rulebook, an Inniscarra player should be the county captain for 2018. But that didn't happen. I don't think they were pleased with Paudie's request to deviate from a process that had existed for years. Several other counties have used a similar structure to appoint a captain. Inniscarra's objection to the switch had nothing to do with me on a personal level, they just felt aggrieved that they wouldn't be able to put one of their players forward for captaincy.

Maybe it's something that was pushed through for me to be that captain that would finally guide us over the line to get that trio of All-Irelands? But in the end, we fell short and didn't even reach the All-Ireland final. We were taken out by a Galway team that had a bit more bite than us on the day.

But I do think that changing the protocol for naming a captain is the system that should be in place. The manager, who has the best insight into how the team operates, should have full control to determine which player will be their general each season. It's the right way to make the selection. That's not to suggest that the club championship method didn't serve the county team well in the past.

A lot of great captains have emerged from the club competition, and I benefited from it in 2007. But, equally, there are other brilliant players who never got that chance because their club didn't win a senior championship during their career, or their club wasn't in Cork's top tier. Their omission had nothing to do with their leadership qualities or their ability to grow into that position.

They simply never got selected because their club team was junior or intermediate, or never progressed past the first or second round of the championship. Relying on that traditional format also means that, sometimes, a player who is not comfortable performing the captain's role, ends up being shoehorned into the job. It's a natural fit for some players but that's not the case for everyone, and the expectations of a captain can become an overwhelming burden. They start overthinking it and that ends up compromising their game.

The current rule for selecting the captain in Cork dictates that the winner of the Cork Senior Championship has first choice on captaincy and they must submit the name of a candidate before a certain date. If they don't make a recommendation before then, the manager is then empowered to make the call. There are probably pros and cons to it, but it's a decision that should be left to the manager. You could have a player who has won a county championship or two, or three, or four. But that player may not be a regular starter for Cork, or maybe they don't get much game time.

And they might not have any other clubmates in the squad who do. I don't think the captain should be a squad player. Your captain must be on the front line, leading the team on the pitch.

Not being an All-Ireland-winning captain doesn't define me, but it would be nice, after playing county camogie from 2002 to '20, to have succeeded in one of those attempts. It just wasn't to be. I know I'm not the only player to suffer this fate. Lots of great players are members of this luckless club. Steph Dunlea, for example, has also been Cork captain twice and, like me, she didn't succeed on either occasion. Hailing from the Cloughduv club, Steph would go through a brick wall for you. A real hard woman.

Still, it's not as if my cupboard is bare.

I HAVE MY All-Ireland medals stored in a box in the home house in Ballyphehane and my All Stars and Player of The Year trophies are in the house I live in with my wife in Boolypatrick. I was selected on 11 All Star teams throughout my 19 years with Cork.

I received my first one in 2004, two years after making my debut, which kickstarted a six in-a-row run of winning All Stars. In 2018, after defending our All-Ireland against Kilkenny, I became the all-time record All Star recipient after collecting my 11th award.

Did I deserve every All Star on that list? I think I earned a lot of them. There was perhaps one year when I was included in the All Star and I felt that was a questionable decision. There was also another year when I didn't make the cut and I was disappointed by the omission.

All Star selections are up for debate every year, and in every code. You could be critical of every team that's selected and I have expressed my dissatisfaction with some of the calls in the past. In 2014, I referred to the All Stars as 'controversial' and said it was disappointing that my Cork teammate Pamela Mackey wasn't deemed worthy of a nomination. Complete agreement over every position is almost impossible to achieve.

I probably don't know enough about the selection process to pick out the exact faults in the system, although I have tried to investigate it by talking to others who have participated in the selection panel.

Every player has their own way of assessing their own performances, and everyone has access to their own stats. If a player crunches the numbers and they add up to a good season for them as an individual, it is frustrating if that's not reflected in the All Star picks. But I don't know if those who are on the selection panel have those stats on hand, or if they use that information when making their choices. But whatever factors are involved in the considerations, the arguments over the All Stars will always persist.

One person's taste is another person's poison. Some people will be fans of one player and others won't be, and I think that plays into it too. Maybe the whole thing is intended to spark conversation and provoke reactions from those who will disagree. I'm not even sure what changes could be made to the system to end all that and ensure a unanimous view.

I'd love to have some treasures from the 2007 and '19 seasons in my locker but All-Ireland titles aren't decided by the opinions of others. No selection panels. No votes cast. There's nothing subjective about earning the right to win… you're either on the higher side of the scoreboard or you're not.

It's definitive, and certainly unanimous.

But you can still feel sore when you don't win. I have lots of medals, but it's normal to feel like there's room for a little more.

CHAPTER 19

FOR THE 2020 SEASON, Paudie tells me that he has different plans in mind for me. I've spent a good chunk of my Cork career playing in the backs and in midfield, but this year, he wants to slot me in at full-forward. The position is not totally alien to me. I actually played in the forwards when I first got onto the Cork team.

In fact, it was in a league game against Kilkenny, when we were short of numbers, that I was redirected to wing-back. From that day on, I spent all of my career between midfield and the backline, with a turn or two among the half-forwards. Paudie loves to experiment with positional switches during the league, and when he was appointed as Cork boss he gave me a run in the forwards.

So, yes, I have some experience of playing in that half of the pitch, but I suppose I haven't played there in the last 10 years. It's not that I don't feel like I could still play at centre-back, but I have gotten older, and you're marking elite forwards who are in their prime. And change is good if you're willing to embrace it.

So, news of this new playing role is exciting for me. It gives me a chance to reinvent my game.

Traditional attackers are hungry score-getters, looking to rack up big tallies. That's not what I'm here to do. I'm not going to be the prototype full-forward. My job is to create havoc in the full-forward line and be a pest to the goalkeeper. I know that I can break down ball for oncoming players and win primary possession to pass off to my teammates.

If I can get a few scores after all that, then happy days.

The project starts off really well, and I'm delivering on all my promises in training and in the challenge games. But now I have a punctured lung the day before our championship starts which has cut my whole season to pieces. I've been robbed of the chance to show my work in big games, and it's just such a pity because I know that with regular practice against the best defenders in the country, I can develop and evolve in this role.

*****

TWO WEEKS AFTER discovering the news about the punctured lung, I meet my respiratory consultant again. He's asking me how I am and I tell him that I'm getting better after finding it hard to breathe at the start.

I mention that the All-Ireland semi-final is coming up soon and tentatively ask if there's a chance that we could aim to get me right for that game? Could I just start doing something gradual that might get me fit in time? He replies that they did a scan, and that he's happy with how it's healing.

He's not quite handing me my hurley and my boots, and opening up the dressing-room door for me, but given the outlook I was facing a few weeks ago, this is a huge reprieve. The medical warnings quickly follow. I'm to do nothing more than a light jog to build it up for now. And no contact training either.

But the possibility of getting back on the pitch is all I'm hearing. That's my focus for the next two weeks. The position I'm in now reminds me of the knee injury I had before the 2017 All-Ireland final, when the six-week recovery window for an MCL tear... I managed to smash out in three.

I have to work a similar trick this time too if I want to whittle an eight-week timeframe down to two.

However, now it's Kilkenny on our own turf in Páirc Uí Chaoimh with a place in the All-Ireland final on offer.

Where there's a will, there has to be a way. I'm just working on slowly building myself back up to make it back in time for the semi-final.

That's what I'm clinging to.

✳

IT'S A MISTY November day when we play against Kilkenny. It's not the typical summer temperatures we're used to on championship days. This is a day for grinding it out, and as we enter the last quarter of the game, myself and Kilkenny's Claire Phelan are in a race for possession out near the wing.

We've had a dream start in this semi-final. I had good, short movement and I wasn't wasting energy by running all over the place. I was planning my runs well and I had my marker Collette Dormer right in the pocket where I wanted her. I scored a goal too.

But we've allowed Kilkenny back into this contest.

Now, it's an arm wrestle to the finish and I'm trying to outrun Phelan for possession. She just shades me for it. I still have a good 20-30 metre sprint in my legs despite being a bit older, but as she fizzes past me, I realise that I just don't have it in me anymore. I can feel that truth pressing against me as the game pushes on for the final stages.

The clock is running out on us... and on my time in a Cork jersey.

I did manage to regain my fitness in time and I was officially named to start at 14 shortly before throw-in. But that's really all the satisfaction I can draw from today.

And that's how it has petered out, in one game, in one season.

Ball burst. Game over.

Kilkenny win by two points to progress to their fifth consecutive All-Ireland final. While for us, 2020 will be our second year in-a-row to miss out on the biggest day of the camogie calendar in Croke Park. That's more like a decade in Cork years.

A famine of a wait by the standards we've set, and the standards which have been set by Cork teams that have gone before us. We were leading by 1-3 to no score after eight minutes, and we completely threw it away. As a group of players, and a management team, we messed up.

It's not for the first or even the second time in my career, but I disagree with how Paudie managed my position in the semi-final against Kilkenny. He decided to take me out of full-forward and move me onto the wing after just coming back from a punctured lung. I was in no position to be out there working the wing. We just lost shape and he should have just left it. He changed it way too early in my opinion.

He made the switch straight after Kilkenny had gotten into the first steps of their rhythm. Teams are always going to get their five or 10-minute purple patch, and that's fine. We just have to ride out that belt of rough weather before the momentum will swing back towards us. But Paudie changed the whole shape of the team and it all fell apart.

And while I was probably grand to play, I don't think I was fit enough for the workload around the middle of the park. That's what I'm feeling now as I look on at Phelan whistling by me in that race for the ball.

I know Paudie complained about some of the refereeing decisions after the game, and I agree that some of the calls were questionable, but really, it was our own fault. We just fell apart and that's unforgivable.

*****

WE'RE ALL PACKED into the dressing-room after losing the 2020 All-Ireland semi-final, and our captain Amy O'Connor is visibly upset as she speaks to us with great passion and emotion. She makes a little dedication to me during her speech, thanking me for everything… saying how she looks up to me, and how she feels that I still have plenty to offer to the group. She later tells me how she was watching me hurl for the Barr's earlier in the year, and how it worried her. She feared that if we succeeded in the club championship, I might get the fulfilment I needed to retire there and then.

She hoped that the promise of another shot at an All-Ireland with Cork would keep me hungry.

It's funny because Amy has spoken about her admiration for me in the past and how she has a signed hurley by me at home from when she was growing up as a Cork supporter. Now, I've shared a dressing-room with her, and watched her blossom into a cornerstone of our attacking force. Amy is such an assured person who knows exactly what she wants in sport, and in life.

She's a talented soccer player who reached the semi-finals of the UEFA European Championships in 2014 with the Republic of Ireland under-19 team. But she had a greater hunger for camogie. She had All-Ireland medals in her eyes from the very first day. She wanted to do pharmacy in college, and she achieved the grades to pursue that profession. Want, want, want… focus, focus, focus. She doesn't drink and she is just so driven. She's developed into one of the main leaders on this team.

BUT EVEN AS I'm listening to her say these lovely words, something strange is happening to me. I feel a sense of peace within me about the result of the game. I kind of surprise myself with how easily I'm processing the blow of being taken out by Kilkenny on our home soil in an All-Ireland semi-final.

My younger self could never accept finishing up like that. But I just feel that time is moving me on. This is not my fight anymore.

Around Christmas time, I go to lunch with two of my Cork teammates, Laura Treacy and Orla Cronin. Still smarting from that loss to Kilkenny, we start planning for the 2021 season. They warn me not to retire.

I tell them I don't know if I can do that, but I also say that I don't know if I can finish off the way we did.

The argument is still raging in my head a bit.

*****

PAUDIE NORMALLY TALKS me around when we have these phone calls. 'Erra, stop talking rubbish and ring me back in a few weeks.'

That's his usual reply whenever I mention the big 'R' word. But this time, he knows I'm serious and doesn't try to dissuade me from following through. Honestly, he probably knew this was coming.

I'm getting a bit emotional on the phone as I deliver the news.

He tells me that he'd have me back in a heartbeat, but he also respects my decision. Paudie accepting that I'm serious about this is making me realise that this is final.

He can almost sense the truth before me.

That respect between us continues to prevail. And everything is still a slag and a laugh with us. Today, in the summer of 2022, I'm walking down Oliver Plunkett Street in Cork city and I can see him sitting outside the Oliver Plunkett bar, quietly enjoying a coffee with some friends, not far from where he works in the South Mall.

I think I'll disturb his peace for a few minutes and knock a bit of craic out of it as I go.

'Howya Paudie, you've aged well,' I shout out, getting the first hit in before he comes back at me with a big swing.

'Oh, Gemma, the weight suits ya!'

Well, that makes it 15-15 in banter tennis.

But how does he like these apples?

'Ah, feck off, Paudie. At least I can lose the weight, but you can't grow any taller than what you are. You're absolutely tiny.'

Game. Set. Match… O'Connor.

EVEN NOW, AFTER both of us have left the Cork squad, there's still good vibes between us. As it was and as it ever shall be. We know exactly where each other's buttons are and we're not afraid to press them. Those bonds don't fade away. We've achieved so much together and his time in charge of Cork makes for absorbing reading. In his 10 years on the throne, Cork contested seven All-Ireland finals, and won four of them. Perhaps we left some titles behind but, all in all, that's a record any manager can be proud of.

He set standards of excellence and we sustained it over the course of a decade. In my time with Cork, the longest stretch we went without an All-Ireland is between 2010 and '13. Since stepping down as Cork camogie manager in 2021, he has gone on to take over the Cork minor hurlers. It's nice to see him link up with that team after coming on as a substitute for Cork in the 1988 All-Ireland minor final against Kilkenny. Hopefully more success awaits him in his managerial career.

The show goes on.

And on.

I'VE ALREADY SPOKEN to Aoife and my brother Glenn about my future with camogie. They're the two main people I want to consult with before making a call. Aoife has always been a massive supporter for me, and would never rush me into finishing up. She would still be in the stands today, if it was my wish to carry on.

Glenn is a bit more concerned about the length of my career. I don't think he was ever telling me to retire but I think he was also getting a bit nervous on my behalf. 'Well now, you have to do x, y and z,' he would say, advising me about how to protect my aging body from the rigorous demands.

I'm just laughing at that, thinking, *Yeah I'm just playing for the last 20 years, I think I'm alright*. But I understand where he's coming from.

And then I just made a decision one day to bite the bullet.

After calling up Paudie to tell him the news, I went about informing my teammates. I didn't want to send one blanket message to the squad, leave WhatsApp groups and just slide away. That wouldn't have been a good enough sign-off in my eyes.

I texted every girl individually to tell them, and I thanked them for everything. As great as people like to think they are, the nine All-Irelands and however many All Stars that I have, it's not possible without any of the girls. I've played with some of those people for a good few years, and some of them are new, and they've all made contributions at different stages. They've all added to it. And 2017 and '18, arguably the greatest achievements of my career, would not have been possible without any of them. And I had different things to say to different people, so I wanted to take the time to articulate that properly to everyone.

AFTER OUR LUNCH-DATE at Christmas, Laura Treacy and Orla Cronin are shocked at the news. But I don't want anyone to ask me to have a rethink or beg me to reconsider.

It's just time to move on.

I have great time for both Laura and Orla, and it's players like them who made playing with this generation so enjoyable. They've often come to me down through the years looking for advice, and now it's their turn to inherit the leadership roles. They are the ones who will lead the charge for Cork from the front lines. The next fleet of players coming off the Cork production line will be going to them for advice.

Laura normally plays at full-back for Cork but has since made the transition to centre-back, which is a tricky switch to make. Full-back is a total man-marking position, where you're consumed by the responsibility of following your marker around the place and not giving them an inch. Playing at 6 is a different prospect, and you have a bunch of different duties to take on. You're obviously trying to stop your opponent and create a stop-gap down the middle to hold them up. You're trying to win possession and be more involved in the game. You also have to be clever with where you hit the ball to create chances.

I've played at centre-back, but never on the edge of the square so I can't even fathom the challenge that Laura is facing.

We've become great friends down through the years. She's much younger and she's not someone I'd be meeting up with at the weekends socially, but I suppose there's massive respect between us. She is someone who has always wanted to do the right thing for Cork, and is always willing to work hard. We always had a great connection on the pitch, and she had a front row seat to myself and Aoife Murray chawing at each other during games. The scars of that trauma will probably never fully heal!

She has often told me how she hated seeing Paudie move me out of position whenever he was experimenting with the team's formation. You and me both, girl!

She's just a great player and a really nice person.

She sent a text to me after she wore the No 6 jersey for the first time. *I hope I did the jersey proud,'* she wrote to me. It was such a humbling message to receive, although she added that she wasn't happy with how she played.

I just reassured her that she's moving really well, and emphasised the importance of forming those triangles with the players in midfield and always offering yourself as an option. Those are just small things that will help her adapt to her new surroundings. She doesn't need to worry. She's a worthy recipient of the 6 shirt.

It's important for Cork to be able to do that without me. And they're already doing that. They've already reached two All-Ireland finals without me. I've been part of the Cork team for so long and while experience is important, sometimes it can be a bit of a crutch for the younger people to think that... *Gemma is there and she'll take charge of a game if we're in trouble.*

I still feel like I could play for Cork and sometimes, when you're part of a team, you feel like you own it. This is our team, our creation... our property.

It starts and ends with us.

You almost forget about the players who preceded you and you certainly don't consider the younger talents that will be coming up after you. The ones who will inevitably replace you. Of course, you never think about that until you must. The wheel keeps on turning.

There's a saying in the army, *'You're only nothing but a number,'* and it's the same in sport. No matter how good you are or how s**t you are, you're only a number. Everything moves on. So must Cork… and so must I.

WHEN THEY REACH the All-Ireland final in 2021, I'm sitting down with the rest of the fans rather than standing on the pitch with the rest of the players. The day you make that switch from the grass to the seat is a hard one.

I take up my seat somewhere between the '45' and midfield mark of the pitch. In this great big theatre of sport. I look out at the teams marching behind the band as the crowd starts getting charged up for the battle of Cork and Galway, and I feel like I can almost put my hand out and touch the players as they pass by. To be watching rather than hurling is a bit emotional and surreal.

Galway are awesome today and they outrun Cork. That's a rare sight but Galway are full value for their victory. They've really done their homework to get things right. When teams dominate for years, it's up to someone else to set the bar and Galway have done that. Now they're the standard bearers.

I've been anticipating this Galway uprising and they have delivered. They're no longer a march behind Cork and Kilkenny.

I didn't exactly plan to publicly announce my retirement through an interview, but that's how things transpired. Linda Mellerick – a former Cork camogie player and now a sports journalist – asked me to do a piece for the local paper, and as I oblige her with just a general chat, she asks me about my plans for the future. The interview coincides with me telling Paudie and the gang, so I decide to let her know too.

There have been so many references to retirement in previous interviews with me over the years. That's because I've been asked about retirement so many times… and whether or not I would be going back for another year?

And then I used to think to myself, messing, *Should I retire? Am I that bad?*

*****

BURNOUT IS A major factor when accepting that it's time to retire. And it's a mental state of fatigue as much as a physical one. It's about admitting that I don't want to be at training and that I'd rather be doing something else with my time. It's about realising that it's okay to say that I'd rather go out and have a few pints and a bag of chips, instead of committing myself to sport at that level for any longer than I have.

Matthew Twomey succeeded Paudie as the Cork manager after the 2021 season, and when he was appointed, he approached me to talk about returning to the Cork panel. I have great time for Matthew… he was a massive part of Paudie's backroom team. But his invitation doesn't appeal to me. He knows that Aoife and I are getting married, and as part of his pitch to get me back, he says that I can take time off for my wedding and rejoin the Cork panel after the break.

But that offer does nothing for me. I've just reached a point where I no longer want to fit my life around camogie. I want to get married, enjoy myself and give my time to Aoife. I don't want to be worried about going back to training next week, and laying off the food or drink at our reception.

I've been maxing it out from November to September since making my debut in 2002. And the pre-season period seems to get shorter and shorter every year. It just becomes mentally draining. It's stressful too.

Even in the pre-season when you're a bit more flexible and lenient with your time, it's still quite a strict lifestyle. You're half-dreading it over the Christmas break because you think that you'll be made to pay for the festive indulgence when training kicks off again. I've always been definitive about deciding whether or not to commit to something.

When I'm back, *I'm back*… and it's 100 percent, and if I'm not, then I'm not at all. There's no half-arseing in between. I won't say that I'll be back and then not show my face. I've just had enough of that and I decided that this chapter of my life is for me and my wife Aoife. Camogie doesn't fit in that way anymore.

I THOUGHT I had retired from the club game too, but I still have a bit of juice left in the tank for my Blues in the Barr's.

There's a familiar face this year in the Barr's management… Paudie Murray. There is just no escaping the presence of Paudie. The constant itch I cannot scratch. He's not letting me slip away without a fight either. Our familiar jigs and reels.

Fellow Barr's man Brian O'Sullivan is part of the backroom team and he's an excellent mentor. He's been involved with our club over the last few years. He defected to the senior hurlers last year which was a bit of a disappointment, but he's back with the camogie outfit again.

'Yerra, g'way... I'll give you a bell in two weeks' time.'

I thought I was done with camogie, but I just can't wriggle free from Paudie's grip and he eventually grinds me down to get back into the ring.

Maybe I'll be in Paudie's position some day, pleading with a player to reconsider their future because I know they have more in the tank? It's not something I'm going to rush into now but I would like to pursue a career in coaching. I still want to be involved with my club or with Cork. Hopefully it'll happen sooner rather than later, but I would definitely enjoy that.

Decisions of this magnitude always make you fear that this could be a mistake, and you question whether or not you're doing the right thing by walking away. That became evident to me when news of my Cork exit began circulating on Twitter. That's when it became public and you're laughing like, *Well, I definitely have to follow through with it now.*

It's nice to see people write good things about you and let you know how much of an impact you had, not just on Cork camogie, but on wider Cork GAA circles. The amount of men who came up to thank me for what I've done for Cork, that was really gratifying. You'd be lying if you said things like that don't matter, especially if anyone says anything sh***y about you. But, thankfully, the reaction was all really positive.

Former players have been in touch to congratulate me on my career, which just shows that players can put rivalries to one side and show respect for their opponents. At the end of it all, as players, we're all bound by a common love for camogie and we're on the pitch for the same purpose. The only difference is we serve different masters. It's nice to have those moments when we drop the guard and salute someone who shares an equal love for camogie when their term of service is up.

While my retirement feels like a mournful time in one sense, it's also giving me a chance to appreciate how far the impact of my career has stretched across my great county. Lots of random people I don't know have sent messages to me too.

I'M CALLING INTO a garage to get the NCT for my car, when one of the mechanics pops out to say hello. 'I just want to say thanks for everything you've done for Cork,' he says to me. This guy is a total stranger and I'm shocked to hear that he even knows who I am, much less feels compelled to tell me something like that.

That was such an unexpected and lovely gesture that reminds me why I gave myself to this life. There mightn't be great crowds at the games compared to other sports, but there's always people watching or following in some other capacity. We forget about that sometimes.

Yes, we'd love to have bigger attendances, and the work to achieve that is ongoing, but people do know about us through reading the newspaper and watching games on TV. There are other ways for people to follow the games.

I know that I chose this life, but as athletes, we still commit ourselves to the jersey and to the game for a long time. You put yourself out there to try and achieve something, and it's only right that people acknowledge your effort. And I always wanted to learn more about how I could better myself as a player.

I maintained that appetite right up until the final few years of my Cork career, when I asked Kevin Murray to help me with my lift. I felt my technique wasn't quite right and I was too low with my lift. You can always seek improvement in your art, regardless of what you've achieved already, or how many years you've racked up at the elite level.

AS IT TURNED out, myself and Kilkenny's Anne Dalton ended up retiring from county camogie within about a month of each other. We've known each other for a long time and we have nothing but respect for each other.

We're both very competitive and there would be plenty of slagging too. She sent me some lovely messages and I obviously contacted her when she retired. That's what it's about. I can acknowledge that she is one of the best camogie players in the game and likewise, the things she said to me were nice.

It's nice that players from different counties appreciate you. It's nice to be nice and it's nice to be truthful and honest with each other, and to form relationships with people from outside your own county.

All Star trips are a great opportunity to do things like that. They allow you to engage with players who you've always just known as your rivals. The first camogie All Stars trip was organised in 2017, when we were brought out to Madrid. We were off again two years later to New York. And while I know Anne Dalton, I got to know other people through those trips and that's why they're important.

They're not just an excuse for a holiday. It's an opportunity to get to know opponents, and realise that they're humans. There are people behind those jerseys.

I always remember Miriam Walsh of Kilkenny out in Madrid and she was like, 'Jesus, Gemma, you're a sound auld skin, really. I didn't think you were that sound'. I was roaring laughing, thinking, *They must have awful things to say about me.*

So, it's important to have the craic with your opponents. Those are some of the memories I can take with me into retirement.

*****

THE DOUBTS STILL lingered, but it was no surprise that I retired because I was at that age to step away. I know that if I went back to Cork training in the morning, I'd probably die on my feet. Once it's gone… *it's gone.*

This way, I get to make my exit on my terms.

I can walk away with my nine All-Ireland titles, my 11 All Stars and my two Player of the Year awards. I can leave knowing that I was never dropped during my 19 years with Cork. I worked my socks off to earn my place on the team and keep my grip of the jersey. Thankfully, the pain of getting dropped just isn't something that I know. Retirement is about knowing the cut-off time, so I'll never have to know that agony now. But you are always wary of the competition for places. It was never a given that I would be starting every day for Cork.

And that's part of why you retire, because you always have those things in the back of your mind. I grew up wanting to play at a certain level, and now I can keep that promise to my younger self. I've played with the great Donoughmore ladies during a golden period in which they won 13 senior county titles, and briefly trained under the brilliant Éamonn Ryan, who has sadly since passed away.

CAMOGIE IS CHANGING and the world of sport is changing. Sport science has revolutionised everything through the introduction of apps and various other technologies that help athletes get a more accurate reading of where they're at, where they need to be and how to get there. It would have been nice to have a little bit of it during my own career, particularly as I was advancing through my twenties and maturing as a player.

You're getting fitter, faster, stronger... and having all that additional help can elevate you even more. There's a new attitude to training practices too. Cork's training was always that bit more advanced compared to other counties, but by today's standards, it was still one-dimensional in my days. It was definitely a case of one shoe fits all.

Now, you still have drills that everyone does together as a team, but there are certain runs devised for the forwards, and other stuff for the backs and midfielders. And then people who have injuries are doing a separate programme. Players are broken into pods doing different forms of training.

Tailoring the work to the needs of the players is the best way forward. What's the point of a corner-forward doing stuff that's more applicable to a back or a midfielder?

I think the timing of the Covid pandemic has helped with my decision to retire too. No one could go to games, and we were all watching them on live streams. That 2020 GAA season seemed to only exist through a screen during that time. If this happened in a normal season, with all of the trappings of a regular season happening all around me, it might have been a different experience.

But you still have to step outside the circle and never return.

You're part of it one day, and everything about you is Cork camogie. And then the next minute, it's as if you never even played for Cork. Here one minute... *gone the next.*

It almost feels like you're non-existent.

Only nothing but a number, remember.

I'M STEPPING AWAY at a time when women's sport is entering a new and exciting chapter. The coverage and recognition has been elevated to new levels. I could really feel the roar of the crowd reach louder decibels in the 2017 and '18 All-Ireland finals. It's such a progressive step but, as a consequence, it means that a lot of my career has slipped under the radar.

I can't say it bothered me but it would be nice to be starting off in sport now with all the coverage, the social media factor and the way camogie has evolved. And if you look at television now and the Women's Euros being shown on RTÉ, that's a fantastic addition to the variety of sports you can see on TV. It would be great if this existed throughout my career, but I just have to accept that that's not the time period for me and I belong to another era.

I can't change time.

I've always felt seen and recognised at home in Cork. I've received plenty of fan mail from lots of people… adults and children alike. Clubs have often invited me out to present medals, and people have come up to me in the street for a chat. I get contacted by a lot of people around Christmastime, asking me to sign a hurley that they've bought for their child as a present.

I might be out in the park and somebody might come up to me and ask me to speak to their child. 'Hi, Gemma. This is my daughter and she loves camogie. Can we take a picture with you?' The majority of people involved in GAA around Cork would recognise me and it's nice to be appreciated by your own, for what you've done in your sport.

THAT 2020 COVID All-Ireland title was one I really would have loved to win. It's a short, snappy year and a really intimate scene after winning the final in the run-up to Christmas. I know this probably isn't a popular view, but I kind of like the idea of not having a crowd there because it's time well spent with the team out on the pitch after the final whistle.

Just you and your unit keeping your celebrations tight.

I told myself that I wouldn't watch that All-Ireland final between Kilkenny and Galway, but that plan fell through when I was out with Aoife's family at a bar, and there it was on the big screen. Right in front of me.

Camogie isn't like football or hurling, where the support base is so massive that the sport doesn't suffer when one person doesn't watch the games. And sometimes you don't want to watch the games because being a player can be so consuming that you're too fatigued to take in any more of the sport. But our game needs every eyeball it can get.

We struggle as an organisation, so I always feel that by not watching camogie, I'm not supporting it. I do feel guilty sometimes, and as hard as it is to watch it when we've been knocked out, I do watch.

*****

KILKENNY GO ON to win the 2020 All-Ireland final and the mystery of my lungs is still being investigated. I've been detailed to go overseas with my job in a few months and this condition could prevent me from going.

Obviously, I don't want to be away from home and my new wife, but not going on a tour of duty would affect my contract. That would essentially make me medically unfit to work, and I don't want to go down that road.

I've had another scan which has shown that the nodules have not reduced, meaning I need to see a cardiothoracic surgeon to get a more invasive lung biopsy. But my consultant has reassured me that I'm young, fit and healthy, and that he was between two minds in the first place about sending me to the surgeon.

His advice is to head overseas, and that we can do the scan after I return.

Time to pack my bags!

CHAPTER 21

IT'S 2020 AND THE world has been rocked by the Covid-19 pandemic. Everyone has a job to do while the world tries to figure out how best to combat this serious and life-threatening virus. Our healthcare workers are fighting for us all on the frontline, providing essential medical care to those who contract Covid-19.

The Government, in conjunction with the HSE, makes difficult calls to impose social restrictions to help keep the case numbers down. The public has to play its part too, adhering to those restrictions when they're in place, and isolating from others when they are required to do so.

The Defence Forces have a big role to play in all this as well. Our job is to provide aid to civil authority, which basically means that we're helping the State. It's a similar situation to when natural disasters or floods occur… the State calls for the Defence Forces to help them out, and the Defence Forces deploy whatever assets they can give. The transport group is deployed to make important deliveries to hospitals and vaccination centres. Engineers provide assistance in constructing and setting up Covid screening centres.

My unit in the medical corps is also required to carry out a service at the vaccination centres.

Our first job is swabbing those who are presenting with Covid-19 symptoms to determine whether or not they have the virus.

IT'S 2021, AND it's decided that vaccines are the answer to conquering this global pandemic. And as the vaccinations come, we have been asked to administer the jabs. We head up to the Citywest for a few days to do some training through our own mentors with the army. We're also working with the HSE nurses.

After that, I'm deployed to Páirc Uí Chaoimh with a small crew for a few months. This is obviously a horrible, and surreal experience for everyone. Covid-19 has claimed the lives of so many people and left others with long-lasting side effects. But it is also gratifying for me to know that I have played my part in helping the public.

It's also been a brilliant learning experience working alongside the HSE.

*****

IT'S LATE 2021 AND I'm back in Lebanon again for the first time since 2013.

This is my fourth tour abroad and my second time in Lebanon. My primary role here is to run the Medical Aid Post as part of the 119 Infantry Battalion, where we provide primary health care and emergency treatment. The team I'm in charge of consists of Irish and Polish medics and our camp is called 'Camp Shamrock.'

I'm at an advanced stage in my army career. So far, I can happily say that my experience in the Defence Forces has been a positive one. But unfortunately, that's not the case for everyone. Allegations of abuse towards women in the army are being investigated at the moment. They're coming on the back of a documentary called *Women of Honour*, which is a horrific watch really.

Those cases are ongoing with the Minister of Defence and there's an independent group looking into that at the moment. These issues are coming to light in the Irish Defence Forces because they are also coming to the surface internationally, and there are other military forces trying to stop all this.

There's a regulation in the Defence Forces called 'A7' which is an anti-bullying and anti-harassment policy. We're all guided by that. Bullying and abuse is unacceptable and they're trying to weed all that out. There should be no tolerance for it. Unfortunately, it's after bringing bad things about that culture to light.

The alleged abuse problems are probably related to issues around power and control of what people can get away with, and the accountability of it. We're put in a close environment and we go overseas together. You're not at home, you're living in a camp and everyone there is in an overseas environment.

That's a challenging set of conditions and it can be even more difficult if you're dealing with the wrong people. I can only hope that the events that are being reported now won't happen again in the future.

We're based in the southern part of Lebanon. We have a great relationship with the Lebanese, which has been forged by the estimated 45,000 Irish citizens who have served a tour of duty in Lebanon over the last 40 years. I have a Cork flag hanging in my living quarters which was given to me by one of the Lebanon locals whose name is Ali.

Ali knows every Irish accent and even speaks with an Irish accent himself. He grew up in the company of Irish people. He doesn't know much about life in Cork but he has been working on what we call 'Mingy Street' for the last 20 years and he can name off every county in Ireland. Trades work is massive in Lebanon and has been an important industry here for thousands of years. Ali was 10 years old when the first wave of Irish peace-keeping troops arrived here in 1978. His father wanted to see if he could make some business by working with the UN and that's how they came to own a shop on Mingy Street.

Ali even knows the complicated history of Northern Ireland. It makes sense that he can make *sense* of all that when he too comes from a troubled place. Like many of the other Lebanese locals, he learned to speak English through his association with the Irish Defence Forces.

Mingy Street is essentially a small shopping district in our camp that serves the troops. The shops are run by the 'Mingy Men' and the shops have everything you need while on your tour of duty. We can go there to get a coffee, buy clothes, gadgets, pizza… you name it. Ali is a well-known character on this strip and I'll return that Cork flag to him when my mission is over.

Haggling is a major part of the Mingy Street economy, and we always have the craic while trying to knock a few dollars off the price. You're going down the wrong path if you don't bargain with them or haggle with them.

I'm in a shop on Mingy Street and I've just spotted a training top that takes my fancy. Ali is quoting a price of 30 dollars, and to me, that's just a jumping off point to commence negotiations.

'Arrra, g'way out of that. I'll only take it if you give it to me for 15 or 20 quid.'

'Twenty-five dollars!' comes the reply.

'No... 20 dollars. That's my final offer.'

At this point, with neither of us willing to budge on the final cost price, I know I need to go to DEFCON 1 if I want to get my way.

'Alright, so...' I say, feigning disinterest. 'I'll leave it off.'

But I know that Ali isn't going to refuse a sale and now I have the power.

'Ok, ok... ok, come back. I'll give it to you for 20 dollars.'

The haggling is always good fun and the Mingy men normally agree to make the sale on a reduced rate. Some people don't like haggling but it's good craic, and I enjoy the back and forth type of pricing strategy that goes on. There's always Mingy Men in Lebanon, and they're nearly everywhere the Irish go on peacekeeping missions.

Wherever the Irish go, they tend to follow and that's especially true in Lebanon. In Liberia, there isn't really a Mingy Street, but Mingy Men would come into camp selling various items like jewellery, watches and lots of stuff which they source from the capital city of Monrovia. They would come in and have a stall open for an hour or two. You can buy stuff or get something and put it on the book, and pay at the end.

It's a totally different set-up culture in Chad. Out there, it's just exposure to pure desert and barren terrain for four months. There are no shops around and the locals live in a really poor economy. The local village has the most basic of makeshift stalls selling shawls, bread and things like that. I think I went to one shop in N'Djamena, which is the capital of Chad, where I bought a few essentials like water, chocolate and crisps.

That's all they had and that was the only thing I bought while I was out there. You buy bits and pieces inside the camp and that's it.

WE'RE AT AROUND the halfway point of our trip, coming to the end of March, when we receive word that there's been an accident. A Polish soldier has just fallen from a forklift and is trapped under the machine. Incidents like this are the biggest threat to the safety of soldiers on overseas missions.

A certain amount of vigilance is always required for the possibility of military warfare breaking out, but it's the work-related accidents and road traffic accidents that pose a much bigger danger to the troops. They happen quite regularly, and when they do we're called into action.

For this accident, the ambulance crew safely extracts the patient and brings him into us at the Medical Aid Post. The soldier is in shock, has an open leg wound on his shin and the bone is exposed. Our main priority is to stabilise the patient, stop the blood and maintain his vitals.

Our Polish and Irish medics work brilliantly together to care for the patient and eventually get him transferred to a hospital where he can continue his recovery. This event just underpins the importance of effective teamwork between the different military counterparts.

*****

SIMILAR TO MY 2013 trip to Lebanon, I'm a 'voluntold' recruit again this time. We quickly become familiar with the sights and sounds of local life and culture. Islam is the main religion for the Lebanese and from our camp, we can hear the Muslim call to prayer every day.

It becomes background noise for us as the days pass by, and gradually drifts away until you almost don't notice it at all. Other days, it might catch your attention again if it sounds a bit louder than normal.

Our time here coincides with Ramadan, which is an important pillar of the Islamic faith. Ramadan is a month where Muslims fast every day from dawn until sunset. It's also a period of prayer and reflection. It's important to be respectful to those who observe the fasting ritual and ensure that you're not eating or drinking too much in their presence, or that you're not talking excessively about food around them.

Two of the doctors working with us are from Pakistan and they're both Muslim, which reinforces the need to be conscientious. They were obviously going through Ramadan while we were all working together, which would put them in cranky form sometimes. It's totally understandable to be off colour when you're not getting enough sustenance.

I don't know how I would react to a month of fasting for about 12 hours per day, while also trying to work at the same standard as always. We show the same courtesy to locals who believe in Christianity too.

Islam is an interesting religion and I enjoy learning about it through one of the doctors whom I've become quite close with on this deployment. The doctors on our missions are like civilians in uniform and part of my job as a medical sergeant involves getting them prepared for the work overseas, and helping them understand what to expect when we get to our camp. I was curious about his religion and as we were getting to know each other, I asked him a few questions about the lifestyle of a Muslim. Some of it is really interesting to learn about.

One thing that has puzzled me about the Islamic faith is its position on pork, and why followers of the religion are prohibited from eating it. They would refer to eating the pig as 'haram' which is Arabic for forbidden.

The pork rule is written in the Quran which is their bible text. Muhammad, my doctor friend, explains that, according to Islamic teachings, everything about the pig is unclean and impure. Pigs are like scavengers and they eat everything, which is why Muslims see the animal as a compromised food source. They believe that by eating pork, the impurities pass into the human system, and that, in turn, makes their body impure.

Muhammad also says that Muslims see pigs as quite carcinogenic on account of the food they eat. Pigs live in filth and excrement too, which adds to the unfavourable image associated with swine in the religion of Islam.

To further my education of his life, Muhammad talked me through some of the details surrounding the feud between India and Pakistan and just generally help me to challenge my own prejudices.

Anybody that doesn't know someone from Pakistan or anywhere else in the Middle East, might make the mistake of putting people into boxes and forming misconceptions about their lifestyle. You think they behave in a certain way or do things in a certain way. That is probably one of the most valuable lessons I've gained through working with Muhammad. Yes, he is a very devout Muslim, but he has some modern views on life too.

Their existence is not solely restricted to prayer and wearing the hijab, and having a certain outlook on women. Yes, there is a different view of women which exists in those countries but Muhammad has helped me to understand that that's not always the case. Women aren't always treated like second class citizens in those parts of the world, and that has been a big learning curve for me.

It has been nice to get to know him, and to study how people live from a part of the world that isn't in direct alignment with the western society that I know.

Meeting Muhammad has allowed me to form a more enlightened understanding of the Islamic religion and those who practice it. It's not this strict and brutal regime that we have been led to believe about those countries.

*****

THE TRAVEL ROUTE for these peace-keeping missions is a bit unusual.

There's no queuing at airport security or browsing through duty free. In fact, we're not anywhere near the regular passengers who are boarding commercial flights to head off on their holidays from the different terminals. We take a bus straight out onto the tarmac where we board an aircraft that's just for us.

From there, we fly directly from Dublin to our destination. It's very straightforward. No need for connecting flights. At least it takes away the stress of trying to navigate your own way to an offbeat location. And since we're travelling in the middle of a pandemic, there's lots of quarantining involved under strict rules around movement. Two weeks in Wicklow after the Irish troops assemble, and another two weeks after arriving at our location where we start to mix with our Polish, Hungarian and Maltese colleagues.

We're here in time for Christmas, which can be a lonely experience for a lot of soldiers who are missing home. The 24th of December is the big day for our Polish counterparts, so we cover them on Christmas Eve and then switch over for Christmas Day to have our holiday time.

We try to make it festive too with the lights, decorations, trees and a bit of Kris Kringle. We also get these welfare packs from our families a few days before Christmas that are filled with things like tea, coffee, sweets, papers and training tops. Some people wait to open those on Christmas morning to make it feel a bit more like home. These six-month spells can be difficult for some soldiers and their mental health.

The environment can become very claustrophobic. They feel stuck. There's only so much training you can do and people can get fed up with the monotony of it. People can get depressed quite easily overseas because you can get into a bit of a rut.

There's no alcohol on this trip either, which carries its own demons in my opinion. I can understand that keeping a teetotal environment here helps prevent people from drinking to excess or slipping into bad habits. But I believe that it's important to have alcohol too because it's how we socialise in Ireland. Our lubricant for conversation.

Drinking moderately allows people to let off a bit of steam and have a bit of craic – within limits – if you've had a bad day. When it comes to the end of an overseas trip, the bar and the mess are usually open. The mess is basically a designated area where military personnel can all socialise together.

Each company, or unit and sub-unit, organise their own barbecue and have a few drinks to toast the good work that's been put down. Removing alcohol as an option dampens those celebrations a bit for me.

How you enjoy your tour largely depends on the frame of mind that you come over here with. It's important to be surrounded by a good group of people that you can have a coffee with or a bit of a laugh.

January and February are the hardest months. They're the meat and bones of the trip. But there are lots of things that you can commit yourself to, in order to make time move quicker. There's a load of wild dogs and stuff like that, and they have a nickname called 'Wadi dogs'. In all, I think there's about three dogs in camp and a good few cats roaming around here.

Some of them wander into camp and we've a health and safety officer who also takes on the role of animal focal officer. There's a vet and animal welfare officer in Naqoura as well. So, if we take in a dog, somebody almost takes on the role of adopting the dog for six months, and they walk it and feed it.

I know some people have tried to bring the dogs back home to Ireland after becoming attached to them. I couldn't possibly get involved in taking care of an animal because I'd be heartbroken when the time came to leave camp, and to have to leave the dog behind. There's this one dog that is literally always waiting outside the medical aid post.

So, one of the Polish women has accepted the responsibility of looking after the dog… his name is 'Ghost'. He's lovely and he just follows her around the camp. So, when she leaves, someone else will take on the role of looking after Ghost.

THERE'S A GAA field here as well where people can go for a puckaround.

It's called 'The Field' and it was designed and completed by members of the 47th infantry group in 2015. It's not in great condition but it's there if you want to smack the ball over and back. I brought one hurley, one sliotar and one wallball with me on this trip. Former Limerick hurler Andrew O'Shaughnessy is out here and there's a group of girls who have played at some level, and we'd go out for a few pucks, even if I didn't get to go as much as I'd like. We were hoping to build some kind of wallball here, but it doesn't look like that's going to happen now.

We're using T-Walls at the moment, which are basically like barriers outside of camp. However, they're not really appropriate because they're all broken and have divots in them. So if you hit a wallball off it, and it collides with one of those divots, it goes pinging in the opposite direction.

Normally, we play hurling games, if there's enough gear and playing equipment in camp, but that's not happening this time to keep movement at a minimum and prevent another Covid outbreak. This is an unusual trip, and events are taking a bit longer to organise on account of Covid.

We normally have soccer and volleyball games as well. We played a lot of volleyball during our tour in 2013 against the Finnish. Similar to the Polish and Swedish, they grew up playing volleyball, so they were class at it. There was one girl in particular who was like something out of the Olympics. We were just a load of GAA players trying to play volleyball, so the gulf in standard was obvious.

We were a bit outmatched, but it was great fun to play. We had such good craic with the Finnish women and I've remained friends with one or two of them on Facebook. They'd have these events and have a barbecue and a sauna. And then we'd repay them the favour when they came down to our part of camp to have a barbecue.

We don't encounter too much of a language barrier with the troops we work with who are from other nations. The Maltese, who work with us directly, travelled over here with the Irish Defence Forces as an attachment. They train in Ireland as part of the Maltese Armed Forces, doing cadetships and other forms of military work, so we have a working relationship with them. I've worked with French troops in the past as well, over in Chad, and also during my last trip to Lebanon.

We were working with them in a more indirect capacity that time, doing medical exercises. We worked with the Swedish directly in Liberia as well. All the troops speak English but their English is learned by the book and very technical. Irish people are very colloquial with the way we speak and we use a lot of slang in our everyday language. We have different dialects and even within the counties like Cork, you have different iterations between places like West Cork and Cork city.

People's language and slang varies, and that can be difficult for soldiers from other countries to understand. Maybe they shouldn't be learning our version of the language, and gaelic slant in our talk. But we knock a bit of craic out of those translations that are slightly off. They might ask what various slang terms mean and they might start using them then.

ONCE FEBRUARY IS finished, you can start to see a bit of a pathway and the end of the trip starts coming into view. The hardest part of these trips is dealing with the unknown. You don't discover what you're going to be doing until you get here. But once I get past that phase and establish a bit of a routine, I hit my stride quite well after that.

We get a visit from the Virgin Media TV station during our deployment. They're here to do a documentary about our work in Lebanon called *Inside Camp Shamrock*. I'm in one of the clips, although you can't quite see me on camera.

It's St Patrick's Day and we've just returned from a patrol to Beirut. I'm in a group of about 20 along with another medic and we're carrying booster vaccines into our camp. We've already experienced a Covid outbreak in the camp but everyone here is already fully vaccinated, all isolation protocols were followed to contain the spread, and nobody became seriously ill with the symptoms.

After everyone gets their jab here, we end up with about 15 surplus booster vaccines, which we have donated to the Cambodia Company and some local Lebanese workers to ensure the vials don't go to waste.

We're coming to the end of our trip and two guys from my unit are organising a fundraiser run. They both have a child who was born prematurely and they didn't know if they were going to survive. There's about 150 of us here, participating in the March For Maternity, and there's an option of doing a 5k, 10k, or 21k run.

I go for the longest one and I have a 14kg loaded weight on my back for the jaunt. It's agony in parts but enjoyable too as I clock a time of two hours and 15 minutes, running most of it with a guy called Ian Delaney from Cork. Initiatives like this help the days tick by when you're coming to the end of a tour. We also had two or three Crossfit Games, Strongman Games and a boxing event.

There were periods where it felt like forever, but overall, I think it did go quickly.

And most importantly, our mission has been a success. My objective as part of the medical personnel is to provide medical assistance for our own troops and for United Nations troops. There must be a medical asset provided for anything involving any unit of the military around the world. It might not be the Hollywood projection of our work, but it's vital and I'm honoured to do my term of service.

*****

IT'S ABOUT THREE o'clock on a Wednesday morning and I've just received a text from Glenn telling me that our aunt Christine has passed away. She was diagnosed with cancer earlier this year but I didn't discover the extent of her illness until recently.

I didn't know that there was a possibility that she could die. Regrettably, I haven't been in much contact with her during my time in Lebanon, but Christine is someone whom everyone in our family has a connection with. She's the youngest of 11 on my father's side, and she has Down Syndrome. She was just such a character.

She used to get the bus to visit us every Sunday morning when we were younger. She was so independent in spite of her condition, bringing a box of cakes with her every time she called in. After dinner, we would drop her back to her home on the northside, where she lived close to mam's mother. She lived with my other aunt, Mary. Her own children became like sisters and brothers to Christine.

I reached out to one of my cousins about Christine when I heard she was sick, and she told me that I could talk to her on WhatsApp.

I just never got a chance to send that message.

I'm down in the gym when I see the text from Glenn about Christine's passing, and I don't really know what to do next. There's only a few days left on the tour and we're at the point where we're conducting the handover with the next crew that's coming over to replace us. I also want to get back home in time for her funeral. But even if I leave now, I'm not sure if I'll make it in time.

I'm supposed to be heading out of camp for the day for work, and even if I decide to leave that off, I'm just going to be stuck here in an enclosed environment with nothing but my thoughts. That's not a great idea with my headspace.

I decide to bring some of the new arrivals out and help them to become familiar with the routes around the area of operations (AO) and show them the ropes.

That will give me some time to make a plan.

I get back to camp and have a chat with one or two of the girls that I'm friendly with, to get their advice on what to do. With all the possible outcomes swirling around in my head, I realise that I'm not going to solve anything here just talking about it. I just have to explain the situation to my bosses and take it from there.

And in fairness, once I make them aware of what's happening with me, they get to work straightaway. They're superb about the whole thing and promise that they'll try and get me home. They're able to reason that family comes first and it's already been such a long trip that there's really no other solution for it.

I hadn't even considered making it back in time for the removal, and I would have made it, were it not for some flight delays. I get out of camp by about 8.45pm to catch a flight from Beirut to Charles De Gaule airport in France, before heading on from there to Dublin. However, there have been delays involved with both flights which force me to miss the removal.

I make it home by Friday evening and get collected by Aoife at the airport. Christine's funeral is on Saturday and her coffin is open in the morning which is so important for me, as it means I can see her one last time.

*****

THERE ARE ABOUT five days left on our trip, but I'm already back in Cork. It's strange for me to finish my peacekeeping mission in these circumstances. I was at a funeral just a few days ago, and today I'm going to a wedding for a cousin on my mam's side of the family. A tragic occasion followed by a happy one in such a short timeframe.

It's such a big pivot of emotion to deal with. I left on the second-last day of the handover and not staying on for the completion of that job feels a bit like my work is unfinished. Once the handover is sorted, the final days of the trip are much more relaxed and I can just take things at a more leisurely pace.

I can do a bit of training, maybe head to the pool or go down to Naqoura for a few days and buy some presents. I'm still around if the new medics need any help with understanding their duties, but otherwise, I'm just winding down.

I organised a separate party for the medics the week before I went home.

We all went down to Naqoura and paid 10 dollars into this kind of resort spot. There was a pool there and we were able to eat normal food there too. At least we all had some kind of send-off as a group before clocking out. But the normal conclusion of an overseas mission is a gradual process. I've missed out on some of that transition out of camp.

There's obviously a good buzz around the camp when it's getting close to home time and even just being around the troops that are coming in to replace us is nice. New faces create a good atmosphere and banter between everyone. On the day you fly back, you dress up in the army uniform and the blue beret for the big homecoming.

The families are all there with their banners and posters to greet us at the airport, waiting for their loved one to appear from behind the sliding doors at the arrivals gate. We're not really a family for making banners, although they did make a concerted effort to put something together for one of the All-Ireland finals.

They got a bed sheet and painted half of it in red to show their support for Cork. It looked more like something belonging to a murder victim in a Freddie Kruger movie.

No, the banners aren't for us, but it is nice to be greeted by your family when you come home from a long trip abroad. You start having the chats and stop off for coffee on the way home, and start looking forward to eating normally again. The main thing I look forward to is a roast dinner.

I always have such a craving for one, so they always make sure to get my carvery ready when I return. It's a bit different on this trip, with Covid still posing a threat, so families have been advised to stay at home this time.

It's exciting to think about coming back to live normally again and get out of the regimented routine. I didn't travel with the group, and instead made the journey home by myself in a civilian capacity. I was coming straight home to a funeral and it was all very surreal. It takes time to hit your stride again even after a regular tour, but everything that's been happening in the last few days has pushed my emotions even further out of shape.

CHAPTER 22

I'M IN THE car with Aoife, heading out towards Heir Island in West Cork, and former Waterford hurler John Mullane is talking to me through the radio. He's frantically giving me a blow-by-blow of what sounds like the game of the century.

This is a match for the ages, and I'm missing it.

Mullane is having heart failure on RTÉ Radio 1 at every breathless passage of play, but I can't see any of it. His animated commentary is all I have to form pictures in my head. It's no use. I'm trying to stream the game on my phone but the coverage is patchy as the car rolls on towards out of service areas in West Cork.

Right now, I want a big TV screen to spring up through the road in front of us and show me what Mullane is talking about.

What am I doing here?

THERE WAS ONLY one thing I wanted to do today… watch Limerick vs Kilkenny in the 2022 All-Ireland hurling final. The football and hurling championships normally conclude in September but the GAA calendar has received a major overhaul this year, effectively splitting the season in half.

The first six months have been allocated to the county games, culminating in All-Ireland finals across July. The second period has been exclusively squared off for club activity. Limerick are aiming for a three in-row today and Kilkenny are out to lift the Liam MacCarthy cup for the first time since 2015.

Mullane, who is famously known for his excited commentary style on the radio, is telling me that it's a cracker. But I'm stuck in this car.

Aoife's sister is down in Heir Island and we've decided to head down and join them. It was a spontaneous call that is now coming between me and the action going down in Croke Park.

'I can't believe I'm missing this!' I snap, even though I knew the risks before I agreed to go.

'Can you stop giving out, please? We're on the way now!'

Aoife's right. There's no point complaining at this point.

We pull into Drimoleague and I dash to the nearest pub to catch the last 20 minutes of the game. I get there in time for Limerick's coronation, while Aoife decides to have a browse around the shops. Limerick are such a supreme machine and they've just capped off their third consecutive All-Ireland title by defeating the hurling superpower of Kilkenny.

Now I can see what Mullane was having a canary about on the radio. After watching most of the final through only his ears, I've scratched the itch and seen some of their glory for myself. Now, I can enjoy the rest of our trip to Heir Island.

*****

PEOPLE ARE ALWAYS fascinated by my love of West Cork. They can't figure out where my attachment to that neck of the world comes from. It's so far removed from the city life that I have been reared in. It doesn't seem to add up for them.

And I don't just visit the area from time to time, either. Aoife and I hop in the car whenever we can to make the journey out that direction. It's our chill zone down there. It's nice for people to have a place that they can keep going back to whenever they need to unwind, and reset. There are places like that all over Cork, and for Aoife's family... Heir Island in West Cork is their sanctuary.

Heir Island is right on the tip of the Cork coast, about an hour and a half from Cork city. If Mizen Head is the most southern point in Ireland, Heir Island isn't far off earning that title. Getting there involves driving down to Cunnamore Pier, which is close to Skibbereen... then catching the short four-minute ferry out to the island.

A return ticket is six quid, which is basically as cheap as a bus fare.

The ferry is a small boat and by the time you get comfy in your seat, it's time to hop up and step onto the island. Aoife's grandmother Máire Ban is a gaelgeoir and she began the West Cork trend in the family when she started going down there on her holidays. She put down some roots when she bought a cottage there some time later, and other members of the family followed her example.

Aoife's aunt and uncle bought houses on Heir Island too, while Aoife's dad built a house on the island. That's how the Ní Chrulaoí clan began their association with Heir Island and the wider West Cork region. And they've just kept it going through the years.

That's the sentimental reason for why we love to go to West Cork, but to answer the question of what's actually down there? Nothing.

Absolutely nothing.

In a place as isolated as this, people either love it or they quickly discover that it's not for them. There's no shop, no bar, no restaurants (until the Island Cottage reopens every summer)… and the population is about 10 to 15 locals who are Heir Island born and bred. Most of the residents, like Aoife's family, are people who live there but aren't from there. They are what we call blow-ins.

And they come from all over the world to find their place on Heir Island. I suppose when you get sick of a life of excess and consumerism on the mainland, this spot is as good as any to cleanse all that out of you.

It's small, it's quaint, it's secluded… and it's quiet.

It's beautiful too.

There's a sailing school on Heir Island that sells coffee during the summer, and there's a lovely pizzeria called 'PizzHeiria' which makes really good grub. People can rent houses and cottages on Heir Island too. There's some nice beaches around the region.

Heir Island is a popular spot among the creative and artistic types. Lots of painters live around here, and in fairness, there are some spectacular sights that are worth capturing on canvas.

If Aoife and I are heading out to the island for a couple of days, we will organise to have food delivered ahead of our arrival. There's a SuperValu in Skibbereen, and with the use of an app, Aoife selects the bits and pieces we need for the trip, and the delivery is waiting for us when we get there. We have all our provisions, but this is the other thing that I love about Heir Island… every day is different here.

You might wake up on Heir Island and head out for a run or a walk. Even now that I'm retired from camogie, I still want to maintain some exercise in my life. I don't think I'll ever stop being active if I can help it. I don't need the goal of winning an All-Ireland to keep me motivated for that.

Sonia O'Sullivan, the Olympic silver medallist who we have the privilege of claiming as a great Cork woman, sums this up really well. She's one of Ireland's greatest-ever athletes who has competed against some of the best long-distance runners of all time. But although she doesn't run at that level anymore, she doesn't need the thrill of a big stage to put on her runners. She just keeps doing it because she loves it and that resonates with me.

I just enjoy gym work and it's not because I have something competitive to focus on. I don't have any inter-county games to prepare for any more but I still love fitness work. And, as I'm getting older and becoming conscious of my body changing, it's probably for my own benefit that I want to keep in some kind of shape.

I do enjoy going for a run here and there too. It's something I won't stop doing… I don't have to hand in my badge as an athlete just because I'm a retired camogie player.

DOWN ON HEIR Island, you just go in whatever direction the day is moving you towards. I have a paddle board here if we decide to head out on the water on a nice day when it's not too windy. We can rent out kayaks if we fancy something different as well.

We have food in for tonight, and the plan is to head over to Aoife's dad's place tomorrow for dinner. But we've just arrived and her uncle, who collected us from the ferry before dropping us off at Aoife's aunt's place, has invited us to eat at his house. That diversion brings us to a céilí in the boathouse on the island, and ends in a great night out.

We're catching the end of a music week here which is a random change of events, but it's great craic. These unexpected switch-ups make our trips to West Cork so enjoyable.

We cover a lot of ground during our stays out here.

Some days, we might head back to the mainland and head out to Baltimore for pizza and a beer, or maybe end up on Cape Clear Island to do a bit of sailing on a lobster boat owned by one of Aoife's uncles. In another spontaneous move, we could head towards Ballydehob or Schull.

And there are other islands to venture to down here. On another day, we're packing up the car to head to Bere Island for a two-day camping trip. Located in the Beara Peninsula of West Cork at the entrance to Bantry Bay, the ferry port is about a two-hour drive from Cork city. It's bigger than Heir Island, and the ferry is bigger too… large enough to bring our car out for the duration of our stay. There's a shop, a café and a pub here.

Aoife's grandmother's family originally comes from Bere Island. Her great, great grandfather was in prison there for a year. He had been interned for the crime of being a teacher in a hedge school. There's a strong military history on the island and the Irish Defence Forces has a barracks there. British soldiers were originally posted on the island and now it's used as a spot to conduct army training camps. The RDF (Reserve Defence Forces) go down there every now and then as well.

As we make our way over on the ferry crossing, I'm thinking that I might see some familiar faces during our stay. An island off the south of Ireland is as removed from modern life as you could possibly imagine, but the world is a town. My prediction turns out to be true, but with a bit of a twist.

The person I end up bumping into isn't one of my army connections.

I'm standing at the bar on the second night of our trip, when a girl taps me on the shoulder. It turns out to be former Dublin camogie player Eimear Brannigan. Aoife and I end up spending the evening with Eimear and her friends, having a few drinks. Her connection to the island is that her grandfather was in the army here, and her sister has a house on the island as well. Come to West Cork for the scenery and serenity, but stay for the pints with a fellow former camogie player.

Some people might find the pace of life is too boring down here. Even with those little unexpected meetings with people you know, and the unpredictable swings in the day-to-day activities, it's just not enough to keep some people interested. And no, it's not a thrill seeker's paradise down here.

There's no bright lights or big sight-seeing landmarks.

But that's not what we're here for. I love the remoteness and the quietness of the area. It's a great spot for me. And it can be a great escape for anyone, if you're willing to slow things down and buy into the simple way of life here.

Maybe nothing extraordinary happens here, but some of the most extraordinary moments of my life have taken place here. This is one of the first places that Aoife and I visited as a couple… the setting of our famous cheese and wine evening.

She trusted me enough to let me into an important part of her world… to check the fit, and see if I could align with it. Thankfully, for both of us, the pieces of our lives slotted into each other with ease.

It's a special place for us.

And if it's significant to Aoife and her family, then it's significant to me.

Gemma and Aoife under a guard of honour during their wedding in Dromquinna Manor and (right) relaxing together.

Despite considering a full retirement from the game, Gemma listened to Paudie Murray one more time and continued to play where it all began, with her beloved Barr's.

EPILOGUE

A LIGHT FLASHES as I place the award on the gravestone.

Right on the second, as I pull my hand away. One movement follows the other so fluidly. It's winter time in 2015 and the dusk is drawing in.

I'm carrying the Player of the Year trophy I received at the All Stars as I walk into Rathcooney cemetery. There's a lamp with a cross inside, sitting at your resting place, and it's burning with a strong flame.

I can still hear your voice booming from the sideline.

I can still see you roaring in the encouragement, with your tracksuit on and your socks pulled up. Your face in the crowd that I could always find in the stands.

The phone-calls on the morning of an All-Ireland final and your honest reviews of every game I played. That warm feeling of relief when you were impressed with how I played… and your little gentle ways of telling me that this was an off-day for me.

The puckabouts in Stiofáin Naofa where we put the building blocks together, and our day out at the Regional Park in Ballincollig where your illness gave you a break from the pain.

Questioning how sport could matter when your light was fading and finally coming to realise its importance because everything I do in camogie means everything to you.

Everything was a 'Hi, girl' and a big smile when you were around.

A hug and a kiss with every greeting.

A love so unconditional for your kids that you could never give out to Glenn and myself, even when you tried. There was no room for coldness in a heart that was always so warm. I could never be in want of anything because you gave us everything.

We talked every day.

And even if a few days passed by without a word or a visit, our relationship never changed. I can still talk to you here, even if you can't reply.

I'm walking in the door of my aunt or nan's house and I can see your face light up as you see me walking in. Always so caring and loving to your family.

Maybe it's just the time of the evening for those holy lights to come to life. If I turn around, I'll probably see a glow from every grave as the night sets in on the cemetery, and the little solar lamps come on.

Candles in the dark for every soul here.

There might be no connection in the timing at all. Setting the award down as the cross starts to flicker in its bright red colour could be proof of nothing.

It could be just that time of the evening causing a happy coincidence.

Maybe it's your wink of approval... 'You were awesome, girl'.

Whatever is happening, I can feel the presence of something spiritual. The flame of your passion for camogie now burns through me.

Your fingerprints are on this award.

All over it.

I was considering a year out from camogie this year, but knowing that me playing would bring you relief in a time of pain, I couldn't walk away. It was all I could do to comfort you.

And this is the culmination of all that.

It all starts with you.

MORE

GREAT

SPORTS BOOKS

FROM

HEROBOOKS